Folklife

ANNUAL 1986

A Publication of the

AMERICAN FOLKLIFE CENTER

at the LIBRARY OF CONGRESS

Edited by Alan Jabbour and James Hardin

LIBRARY OF CONGRESS · WASHINGTON · 1987

Folklife Annual *presents a yearly collection of articles on the traditional expressive life and culture of the United States. The articles are written by specialists in folklife and related fields, but the annual is intended for a wide audience. A publication of the American Folklife Center at the Library of Congress,* Folklife Annual *seeks to promote the documentation and study of American folklife, share the traditions, values, and activities of American folk culture, and serve as a national forum for the discussion of ideas and issues in folklore and folklife.*

The editors will consider for publication articles on all areas of folklife and are particularly interested in the folklife of the United States. Manuscripts should be typewritten, double-spaced, and in accord with the Chicago Manual of Style. *Submit to: The Editors,* Folklife Annual, *Publishing Office, Library of Congress, Washington, D.C. 20540*

CORRECTION:
In Folklife Annual 1985, *on page 148, the photograph* bottom left *was incorrectly identified as "Tower for the Brooklyn festival." The tower shown is one from the Nola festival in Italy.*

For sale by the Superintendent of Documents, U.S. Government Printing Office, Washington, D.C. 20402
ISBN 0-8444-0514-0
ISSN 0747-5322

Designed by Adrianne Onderdonk Dudden

Contents

Editors' Notes

One of the purposes of *Folklife Annual* is to provide a forum for the discussion of theories and procedures of folklife study, and the editors believe that such discussions gain special importance as the hundredth anniversary of the American Folklore Society approaches. The communities of people that are depicted in the 1986 annual include teenagers in New York City, Peruvian Indians on the slopes of the Andes, and Finns in their homeland and in America. In bringing these essays together the editors intend to demonstrate both the variety of folklife communities and the unexpected similarities displayed by seemingly disparate groups or situations. We discovered also that the essays exhibited a commonality we did not anticipate, for each one presents an encounter between two groups within a society or, more to the point, between an outside observer-researcher and the community observed: Elias Lönnrot seeking out a national tradition in the tales of rural "singers," Sally Banes or John Cohen photographing teenage breakdancers or South American Indians, William Wilson helping to present publicly sponsored folklife programs, or Russell Lee documenting life in a Minnesota lumber camp in the 1930s. In each case the photographer or folklorist cannot discount the effect of his or her own involvement with the community observed or the material studied.

This fact is dramatically (even dangerously) apparent in the work of Sally Banes and John Cohen, but many who have done fieldwork, even of a less exciting variety, will see their experiences and problems reflected in the essays here. Few communities are isolated enough to be free of impingement—particularly in America where radio, television, public education, and popular culture are nearly universal. Sally Banes's essay provides a case in point. But in addition to recognizing the difficulty of identifying a "pure" community or tradition, folklorists need to consider both their own attitudes toward the people and material they study and the way they themselves are regarded by their subjects. The folklorist is neither anonymous in the material he gathers nor invisible to the people he studies.

Folklife is the study of tradition, of course, of what carries forward through time, providing continuity and identity with a place or an activity. But also emerging from the essays in the second volume of *Folklife Annual* is a sense of the forces of change—in Finland or Peru or on the streets of New York City. Arvid Asplund's life changed for the better when he married and began a family of his own, although it was his early life that he judged most important in telling his "life story." He sent in "Via Dolorosa" in response to a notice inviting manuscripts for this annual. The editors wish to thank Gerald E. Parsons, reference librarian in the Archive of Folk Culture, for organizing the symposium of commentaries that follows it and thus showing us how best to present Mr. Asplund's story. Since the essay grew out of a writing class, we did not treat it as an "artifact": some light editing was employed for such matters as capitalization and spelling; section breaks were supplied. But the style, like the choice and arrangement of topics, is Mr. Asplund's own.

JH

Llamas of the Qeros. Photograph by Emilio Rodriguez

Breakdancing

A Reporter's Story

BY SALLY BANES

PHOTOGRAPHS BY MARTHA COOPER

Breakdancing is a craze that has easily surpassed the twist for media attention and wildfire popular diffusion—its energy and ambition seem to symbolize the 1980s. It is also a richly complex phenomenon to examine. First, breakdancing is not an isolated form of expression but is integrally linked to rapping (a form of chanted poetry descended from black oratory), scratching (the music made from record-mixing techniques), subway graffiti, slang, and clothing fashion. To study breakdancing is to study an entire energetic urban adolescent subculture called hip-hop, that has spread from New York City black and Latin ghettos across the United States and beyond the Americas to Europe, Asia, Africa, and Australia. And to analyze breakdancing and hip-hop is also to consider the ways in which the spread of that subculture has inevitably

Breakdancing on the Upper West Side of New York City

fragmented and distorted it and to note how the popular global media serve as both imagery for and agent of hip-hop culture. Second, because breakdancing builds its unique style on the solid foundations of the Afro-American dance repertory, it opens a window not only on the present youth culture but also on the history of black dance on both sides of the Atlantic. Its study sheds light as well on the continuous process by which folk dance is transmuted into theatrical dance and vice versa. And further, in terms of its own short history, breakdancing is particularly compelling because new generations of dancers arise so quickly on the heels of the old. The telescopic story of its permutations and transformations, as well as its tenacity and flexibility in the face of various changes, lets us observe the vicissitudes of an oral tradition in an incredibly short time span. And finally, partly because of its close relationship with the media, the observers and recorders of the form—

myself included—are willy-nilly participants, since they have had such an enormous effect on its meteoric history.

In the fall of 1980, I received a call from Martha Cooper—a photographer, a visual anthropologist who specializes in children's play, and a working journalist. For several years she had been documenting subway graffiti (her book, *Subway Art*, with Henry Chalfant, was published in 1984). She told me that as a staff photographer for the New York *Post* she had been sent to a police station in Washington Heights the previous winter "to cover a riot." When she got there she found only a few dejected-looking kids who had been arrested for allegedly fighting in the subway when they claimed they were dancing. Marty's interest in them was

Teenagers from the High Times crew being watched by a Department of Transportation officer in a subway station in Washington Heights as they demonstrate moves for New York Post *photographer Martha Cooper after their release from the police station, January 1980*

fueled by seeing the confiscated cans of spray paint and martial arts paraphernalia that marked them as part of the graffiti subculture. According to the kids, the cops had to admit defeat, drop charges, and release them because the kids proved conclusively that they had, in fact, been doing a shared dance. Marty asked them to take her back to the subway station and show her their dancing moves. She photographed them and took down their phone numbers. When she called me, she was just getting around to looking them up and asked if I would be interested in writing an article about this kind of dancing for the *Village Voice* (where I frequently wrote about dance and performance). It was something she'd never seen before—solo performance with wild acrobatics and poses—and she found it hard to describe.

But having a second look turned out to be harder than we bargained for. For one thing, these kids were shy about demonstrating their dancing for adults, even for two encouraging and sympathetic reporters. Their mothers disapproved of their breakdancing indoors, since they invariably knocked into the furniture, and they also disapproved of their breakdancing outdoors, since (although the dancing itself wasn't, after all, fighting) the activity seemed connected to all kinds of illicit behavior and institutions—like graffiti and street gangs. (The word *crew* replaced *gang* when the talk was of graffiti or dancing rather than fighting.) And the competitive nature of the dancing at times did lead, in fact, to actual combat.

A further difficulty for our investigation was that these kids—members of the High Times crew—assured us that this kind of dancing no longer interested them or their friends. It was out of fashion, they insisted. Roller disco was now the going thing. They ran a little karate school in the basement of a neighborhood apartment building, where they finally hesitantly showed us bits and pieces of the form. Even the name hadn't crystallized; when we tried to tell them (and afterwards tell new informants) what it was we wanted to see, they referred to it as "B-Boy," "rocking," "breaking," or even "that kind of dancing you do to rapping."

We recorded some improvised a capella raps and they invited us to several occasions where they thought a jam would materialize, but by Christmas, when we went to the karate school's recital for friends and families, we had yet to reach our elusive goal—to see "the real thing." It occurred to us that perhaps the form was hibernating and would reemerge the next summer in the parks. It also occurred to us that perhaps this was, indeed, a fad that had appeared and already disappeared without attracting mainstream attention and that we'd missed our chance.

But we were determined to satisfy our curiosity before a possible summer revival, and though we continued to search for the form at rap concerts, school dances, and other events, we tried another method: we began to track down more breakdancers by sending out feelers among graffiti writers. Henry Chalfant, Marty's colleague, was planning a slide show of his photographs of subway graffiti at Common Ground, a loft in Soho, to be accompanied by live rap music. When Marty asked him whether the graffiti-writers he knew did breakdancing and Henry discovered that they did, he decided to include that too as part of the show. A crew—Rock Steady—was found, and it promptly split itself into two for the sake of competition. The "fake" crew called itself Breakmasters. We supplied both sides with T-shirts ornamented with crew insignia—"colors" in hip-hop slang, which serve as prizes in real jams, with the winner taking the loser's. At the time the T-shirts and the wide colorful sneaker laces were the most elaborate parts of the breakdancers' outfits. Later, crews developed entire uniforms as well as a style of layering and slashing clothing that formed a visual analog to the mixing and scratching of records by the DJs. Fab Five Freddy (Braithwaite), the graffiti-writer-turned-easel-artist who wrote Blondie's hit song "Rapture" and later would be the musical director of Charlie Ahearn's film *Wild Style*, served as both DJ for the event and knowledgeable informant for us. Ramellzee was the MC—an acronym reworked, in the hip-hop manner, to mean "mike control" or rapper. As they all rehearsed for the upcoming "Graffiti Rock"

Practicing moves in Harlem

show, we photographed, asked questions, and took notes (and even dance instruction); gradually other people dropped by to film and videotape the goings-on.

The form as a whole looked like nothing I'd ever seen before, though it did include very familiar moves. Its spatial level called to mind Capoeira, the spectacular Brazilian dance cum martial art form that incorporates cartwheels, kicks, and feints low to the ground, but the two were dissimilar enough in shape and timing that Capoeira seemed at most only a distant relative, and certainly one the breakdancers weren't acquainted with—at least on a conscious level. There was a Caribbean beat to the rapping and music that most often accompanied the early breakdancing—and rocksteady is a form of music related to reggae—but the dancing, though it shared with Jamaican ska and other Afro-American forms the use of pantomime and narrative capacity, wasn't a close relative of reggae dancing either. Though in certain ways breakdancing as a pastiche of pop culture in the 1970s and 1980s—with its references to TV, *Playboy*, comic books, kung-fu films, and even the spinning turntable—seemed utterly new, in other ways it was clearly a direct descendant of African and Afro-American dance traditions, from its format (a solo performer inside a ring) to its rhythmic structure (syncopated), to its movement vocabulary (the leg wobbles of the Charleston, the acrobatic spins of black dance from Africa to the flash acts of New York nightclubs, the mimed freezes), to its rhetorical modes (the boast and the insult), to its function (male exhibition and competition). It was a distinctive new dance, but one with a solid pedigree.

The term *breakdancing* continued (and continues) to provide food for research. In music, the term refers to brief improvised solos in jazz, often making use of a suspended beat and inventive flourishes. It was exactly the break in swing music that made it "hot." The parallel with breakdancing seems clear. When I first asked kids what *breakdancing* meant, they told me, "It's when you go crazy on the floor," and that it was the change in the musical phrasing that compelled one to break out into the most outrageous possible movements. As Fab Five Freddy put it, "They started going

Taunts, boasts, and insulting gestures are an integral part of breakdancing. Take One's dance movement in this photograph simulates a "befouling" of Frosty Freeze.

Front page of the Village
Voice, *April 22–28, 1981,
which features the article
that broke the story on
breakdancing*

wild when the music got real funky," when
the drummer's beat took over. The term
breakdown refers to both the dance and the
music of a nineteenth-century black ver-
nacular dance, a kind of reel that entered
the white repertory as well—and by extension entered American slang to mean a rau-
cous gathering. But also, the *break* in vodun
is a technical term that refers to the point
of possession in the dancer, controlled by
the playing of the drummer. And further,
in French Guiana a traditional dance is
called, in Creole, *cassé-ko* (breaking the
body). Clearly this linking of ecstatic dancing, suspending the beat, and the term *break*
itself is a continuing idea in Afro-American
dance culture. And further, the various vio-
lent, destructive meanings of the word see
their parallels in the scratching of records
by DJs and the ripping of clothes in hip-
hop fashion.

In April 1981 I wrote the article for the
Village Voice that would serve as the pre-
view for Henry's concert, scheduled for two
performances in early May. The response
to the article was overwhelming. By the following weekend, three extra shows had to
be scheduled and the Rock Steady crew had
performance dates lined up at several summer festivals and filming dates for various
television news specials. In retrospect, it
seems it was that article that introduced
breakdancing aboveground.

But Rock Steady's sudden fame had other
repercussions. Before they could reap their
rewards, they had first to pay for their hu-
bris. After the first of the "Graffiti Rock"
concerts, a rival crew, from Brooklyn, appeared at the performance space and
threatened violence. Rock Steady was an
uptown crew and had overstepped its turf,
though it was never clear whether the Ball-
busters, as this group was called, were rival
dancers or simply fighters. Henry and the
crew members decided to cancel the remaining shows. And our faith in what one
breakdancer had told us—that breakdancing had replaced fighting among street kids—
was shaken.

But the rise of breakdancing, and of the
Rock Steady crew, was already unstoppa-
ble. What began as a folk form, a dance-
game among adolescent boys that symbol-

Above: "Graffiti Rock" television show, starring Michael Holman and the New York Breakers

Right: A member of the group Rock Steady demonstrates breaking for a bemused group of folklorists at a conference on the folk culture of the Bronx, May 1981.

Opposite page, above: Filming for a 1981 show on the television program "20/20," the first of many television shows to feature breakdancing

Opposite page, below: Breakdancers watching themselves on videotape at the Negril, a reggae club in the East Village

Cliff Lyons (Spider) of the Dynamic Rockers in Queens, New York. Now known as the Dynamic Breakers, this crew has elaborated its moves with group choreography, aerial spins, and balletic/acrobatic partnering.

ically asserted various aspects of personal identity and group solidarity, became theatrical and then, in turn, was taken by its younger acolytes back out into the parks and streets. Every new performance situation initiated changes in the form. For instance, a few weeks after the "Graffiti Rock" show, Marty and I presented a paper on breakdancing with slides at a conference on the folklore of the Bronx. Members of the Rock Steady crew, entirely at home behind microphones and in front of a mesmerized audience, served as commentators, and the next day they were given a local roller skating rink to perform in. The space and the equipment inspired them to new heights of invention: breakdancing on roller skates, group choreography, open-field performance. In another few weeks they had already outgrown the status of folk performers as Henry Chalfant and Tony Silver, who had met as a result of the *Voice* article, filmed them competing with a Queens crew, the Dynamic Rockers, in another roller

rink, for the documentary film *Style Wars*, which appeared on PBS in 1983. The logistical needs of the film crew created yet more stylistic changes in the dance form. For example, the man who ran the roller rink kept telling the kids to open up the circle to give the cameraman room. The next time we saw breakdancing in the park—by now people were jamming in parks again—we happened to run into Rock Steady. Crazy Legs, by now president of the crew, was walking along the edge of the circle telling everyone to open up the circle.

The widespread media dissemination not only changed but also for a time homogenized the form. What at first had been moves of idiosyncratic personal style, with imaginative invention at a premium, though firmly rooted in the basic conventions as passed on from older cousin or brother to younger apprentice, were copied ad infinitum and became fashion. At a party the following fall I saw a group of neighborhood kids my host had hired for the eve-

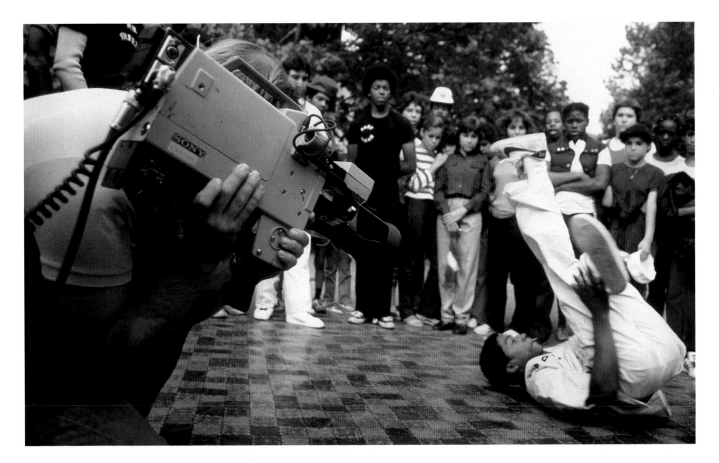

Shooting Charlie Ahearn's movie Wild Style.

Scene from Harry Belafonte's movie Beat Street. *Crews were auditioned at a competition held at the Roxy, and one scene featured a dancing battle between crews in a subway station.*

ning's entertainment and noted their stylistic similarity to the Rock Steady crew; I asked them where they'd learned to breakdance. From seeing it on television, they told me.

Rock Steady began performing regularly at the Negril, a reggae club in the East Village, and refining their choreography with the instant feedback of video as well as audience response; at first Chalfant set up some jobs and then they took on as their manager Kool Lady Blue, who organized hip-hop nights at the Negril, then at the new wave club Danceteria, then at the notorious Roxy. The professionalization of breakdancing had begun: downtown choreographer Julie Fraad organized the Magnificent Force and gave their performances a narrative structure; Michael Holman managed the New York City Breakers; the

Kitchen, a Soho center for avant-garde music, video, and performance, presented an evening of Rock Steady as part of their dance series. The independent filmmaker Charles Ahearn shot *Wild Style,* a musical with a fictional narrative that featured real graffiti writers, rappers, scratchers, and breakdancers. Patty Astor (who in the film plays a white reporter who discovers hip-hop culture as she researches graffiti in the Bronx) opened The Fun House disco. The Hollywood film *Flashdance,* with the Rock Steady crew, came out in the same year, 1983, and though its breakdancing sequences lasted less than two minutes, it made the dance a national phenomenon. *Breakin'* and *Beat Street* followed fast, as did an entire stream of movies that hasn't ended yet. These films documented another phase in the development of breakdancing: its merger with the

West Coast form electric boogie, an upright style (as opposed to the floor-oriented breaking) inspired by robotics (as opposed to the martial arts imagery of breaking).

At the same time, breakdancing as an amateur activity proliferated. By 1984, you could buy several how-to-do-it books as well as even more numerous how-to-do-it videotapes. All over the suburbs, middle-class housewives and professionals could take classes at their local Y's and dance centers. (Much of this instruction, however, centered around electric boogie rather than the more physically demanding breakdancing spins and freezes.) And the road from amateur to professional could often prove a very short one, as kids took to street corners to perform for donations from the crowds of spectators they attracted. The very term *street dancing* had changed its meaning in regard to breakdancing from private to public performance, from folk to theatrical status, from performing for one's peers to performing for money.

The meaning and nature of the competitive element of breakdancing have also taken on new dimensions. In its original, folk form, breakdancing was a dance-game, a cooperative (though not always friendly) competition in which kids tried to top one another in order to win honor and fame (sometimes symbolically expressed in tangible form by the above-mentioned "colors") not only for themselves as individuals but also for their crews. It was in the crucible of the contest that the form's moves were forged. Its vocabulary alluded to fighting in its use of martial arts maneuvers. That combative heat and pressure generated a style that was intricate, witty, raw, and flamboyant—inventive by necessity. The film

Breakin' portrays (albeit in Hollywood fashion) just such a competition, where one senses that the dancing does metaphorically stand for fighting in proving power and virility. (Contrary to the norms of street life, in this movie women also enter into the fray.) As breakdancing became more theatrical, with public performances as exhibitions replacing private performances as interactions, the element of contest re-emerged in a new form. At clubs like the Ritz and the Roxy, crews began to vie for cash prizes and movie roles in contests organized not by the kids themselves but by the club managements or movie producers; they were judged not by their peers but by panels of "expert" judges.

But with the rise of breakdancing on the Hollywood screen, yet another level of competition has appeared—the battle of the dance genres. From *Flashdance* to *Breakin'* to *Beat Street* to *Body Rock*, the plot of the hip-hop movie inevitably takes a crucial turn when the youthful vitality and (literally) down-to-earth quality of the breakdancing is pitted against an entrenched form—ballet or jazz dancing—that is shown as effete, decadent, and creatively exhausted, if not downright offensive. The battle lines are clearly depicted as class lines. And, of course, breakdancing always wins.

Breakdancing was invented by a generation of kids raised on television, movies, radio, and video games. The relationship between the dance form and the mass media is densely layered, beginning with the use of pop culture imagery and with brevity of format, and evolving with the succession of responses to media coverage and dissemination. The very success of the form and of some of the dancers, in fact, seems an American dream-come-true that could only have been concocted in Hollywood. These kids' sensitivity to—and sophistication in the use of—the popular media is essential to the nature and development of this urban folk dance.

Breakdancing moved to
midtown New York in
summer 1981 with its first
mainstream performance at
Lincoln Center.

Among the Qeros
Notes from a Filmmaker

BY JOHN COHEN

It should have been evident that there would be filming problems when the president of the community of Qeros announced in August 1983, "Everything is different now. The Japanese filmmakers have been here. They have paid people individually every time they filmed." I told the president that I was planning to bring sickles for every family in the community to help them clear land in the jungle. I asked him to consider which would be preferable, to pay a few individual families to allow filming or to bring something for all the community. After a night of thinking it over, he said to bring sickles. But the people I know in the hamlet of Wayuna Pampa said that they would "put on a dance for me for one million soles." I told them that I was a human being, not a bank.

The region of Qeros is situated on the

Qeros woman. Photograph by Emilio Rodriguez

east slopes of the Andes in Peru. The four hundred Indians who live there are also called the Qeros, although to themselves they are the *Runa*—the People. They are shepherds of llamas and alpacas, and they live in clusters of stone houses in high valley heads at fourteen thousand feet—just below the snow line. There are about seven Qeros hamlets scattered across the region, which is isolated both culturally and geographically. Above them are snow-covered peaks, and below them the Amazon jungle stretches to the horizon.

I have been visiting Qeros since 1956 and made recordings there in 1964 and a film in 1979. I told the president that I would return in 1984 to film at Carnival, an intense festival for the Andean communities that has little to do with Catholic ceremony but invokes many indigenous beliefs and rituals. In this film I wanted to convey something of the role of music in the context of daily and ritual life, for it seemed so central to understanding the Andean people, and I had received a Guggenheim fellowship to make it, as well as the cooperation of the national airline, AeroPeru.

In 1979 when I received payment from PBS Nova for the leasing of my film "Qeros: The Shape of Survival," I sent $500 to Peru to help pay off the tax debt on Qeros land. The money never got to the people. In 1977, while making the film, I had given axes to all Qeros families (there were eighty of them then) to help clear jungle land to grow corn. I did this under the advice of anthropologist Steven Webster, who had spent several years with the Qeros. The problem of compensation for information, for observation, or for documentation (through film or recordings) has become a difficult issue for tourists, anthropologists, and filmmakers alike. Western civilization, in its curiosity, continues to invade the most sheltered corners of the world in ways that go beyond the usual capitalist expansionist need for new markets.

In February 1984, when I returned to Peru with Peter Getzels, a student of anthropology who was helping me with sound recording, people in Cuzco told us that the Japanese were already in Qeros, preparing to film at Carnival. We were told of their large crew, their special cameraman with the finest Arriflex equipment, their system of sixteen runners who brought them supplies from over the mountains, as well as their mountaineer guides from the north who were now trained to "cook Japanese meals." We heard that television money was behind them, and Peter and I were forced to consider the moral problem caused by TV's powerful resources, which can convert the daily lives of ordinary people into a commodity to be viewed by unseen audiences as a form of entertainment.

One might argue that the discrepancy between the U.S. and the Third World economies is so great that paying for the right to record and document is the only decent thing—in light of the fact that "native peoples" will never get anything else from it. This argument raises questions about the purpose of anthropology, the ethics of doing field work, the nature of tourism, and the potential for exploitation in filmmaking. It points to the deficiencies in our own society, which seeks fulfillment and alternatives in the cultures of others, and calls attention to the evils our system has sometimes wreaked on others. It also evokes feelings of uneasy guilt about the inequality of contrasting societies and individual lives.

Increasingly now tourism in the Third World has become an industry that converts folklore and native culture into commodities. Culture is up for sale, and in Puno, "The Peruvian City of Folklore," every guide is a folklorist, every restaurant performs "authentic music," and city dwellers have become the experts and explainers of country life. While filming a folkloric group at a *bordado* (embroidery) shop, I recognized the dancers as clerks, secretaries, and salesmen from a nearby electronic appliance store. It has become increasingly difficult to get out to the rural communities where traditional practices might still be observed. Indeed, in the small communities, many of the rituals are now performed only at stadiums during touristic festival dates, and thus the internal meaning of the ritual can be called into question.

My own needs as filmmaker are satisfied

by working with poetic and mythic values, and I make films to show the connections between cultures and people. My world has been made richer by shared knowledge, and this knowledge must be handled with ethical delicacy, or else gaining it becomes another form of exploitation. As Peter Getzels explained it, the issue is reciprocity and exploitation. Even in anthropology there is the temptation to fall into certain interactions, which may be done in the name of knowledge but are in fact ethical traps. In his work with the Qeros, Peter had been asked many times to become *compadre* (godfather). He finally agreed for one informant because he knew the man's father had stories to which he could gain access. Peter has learned many Andean ceremonies in order to play the game by Andean rules and thus gain access to the Indians' private thoughts and mental constructs. But he sees the inherent immorality in this activity if it is done only to get a Ph.D.

In my relations with the Qeros, I can often be criticized for not observing, studying, and attending to their everyday ceremonies and rituals, which are many and constant: there is the practice of selecting well-formed coca leaves to make groups of three, breathing upon the leaves while invoking the names of local mountain spirits (Aukis and Apus) before ingesting them, offering coca to the giver, preparing and offering cooked potatoes for a close relationship, or presenting raw potatoes for future use.

Invariably my presence has been an imposition, disrupting a busy schedule of planting, harvesting, herding, weaving, and the making of rituals. The Qeros get nothing from me in return. Yet I hope that they receive compensation in the way my photographs and film work communicate something positive about them to the outside world. On my visits during ceremonial events, I have provided the coca leaves for all sides. Often my gifts are one-directional rather than reciprocal, and I give expecting nothing specific in return. This may be at odds with local custom, and I hope the Qeros can make allowances for my transgressions. Over the years, I too have been called upon to become a *compadre*, which goes along with a haircutting ceremony and the gift of money for the child's future, but re-

cently Peter Getzels has told me that the Qeros are abusing this custom in order to get the gifts. Although this is disquieting information, I can only accept it for what it is. I'm in no position to pass judgment on Qeros motives.

A Personal History

I've been coming to Qeros long enough to witness the changes from the hacienda regime through the land reform of 1972. My first visit there in 1956 was in the company of Eduardo Dubarry, the son of a nearby hacienda owner, and there was no doubt about Qeros deference to this powerful *viracocha* (chief). However, on subsequent trips with majordomos of the hacienda as my guide, the relations between the Qeros and myself changed. The majordomos were feared but less respected, and I found myself more in the role of inquiring curiosity than that of sheltered guest. After the land reform, the majordomos lost their power and were considered merely as mestizos, a class apart, situated above the Qeros but with only echoes of power. And the Qeros perception of them was tinged by a deep resentment. Over the years, however, many majordomos had become *compadres* to the Qeros and thus held that different kind of control over them through obligations.

By 1976 when Emilio Rodriguez and I went to make the Qeros film, we had to develop our own connections with the Qeros. Neither of us spoke Quechua, and we occupied none of the positions they were accustomed to: we weren't mestizos, hacienda representatives, government agents, salesmen, or mining engineers. We neither commanded respect nor made demands on them. We didn't remain standing as they squatted before the mestizo guide, we didn't order them in harsh voices, and we didn't evoke the obsequiousness that was given to the mestizos. We acted the clown, the ignorant traveler, and shared our food and other things with them, although at the same time, and inadvertently, we failed to recognize certain traditional Andean rituals of

John Cohen, 1977. Photo-graph by Emilio Rodri-guez

behavior. Rather, we were a puzzle to them as we sat on the ground with them and shared our sleeping bags, food, and concerns—or so we thought.

The Qeros were curious about our possessions—our watches, wool pants, and down vests—and expressed a proprietary, acquisitive interest in them. They have all these things now: over the years I have watched with dismay as transistor radios have worked their way over the mountains into Qeros homes, bringing messages of Huayno music and advertising along with discarded Ray-O-Vac batteries that slowly rust away as litter on the landscape.

Between my August 1983 and February 1984 visits, something changed radically. The first signals came as we descended from the mountain pass that leads into Qeros. The welcomes were gone and words of warning were everywhere. It felt as if a poison had been spread or some outside force had intervened in our relationship. As we passed a corral by the houses where some people were slaughtering a llama, an unfamiliar Qeros man asked us what right we had to be there. I told him I was bringing sickles for the entire community. "How many?" he asked. I said, "One hundred—enough for all the families." He said, "Leave them all here, we need them." Then he said something in Spanish about becoming a member of the Guardia Civil as he was going to protect the Qeros from outsiders, especially in preparation for Peru's planned highway along the eastern slopes of the Andes just above the jungles where the Qeros are located. He was indeed the son of a Qeros family and had moved away into town. He was now visiting his family for the Carnival celebration. Loaded with the suspicions of the outside world, he asked how much money we were making from the film.

Even my old friend and *comadre* Andrea and her daughter seemed to have masks over their faces, and in the presence of their parents and larger family they appeared not to recognize me. (We had been joking and embracing only six months earlier.) I visited them alone and some of the warmth returned. I asked about the baby I was *compadre* to, who had laughed when they sang to her in the film, and learned that the baby was dead. All winter long as I edited the film of the previous visit, the image of that baby and her surrounding family had communicated life, warmth, and smiles to me. Suddenly I couldn't stop my tears, for this hit me hard. Later I was told that Andrea was disturbed that I had not accepted a gift of potatoes she had made for me the previous year. Probably I wasn't hungry at the time, but I had broken an important Andean tradition by not accepting food.

A Warning

We were warned not to descend to the Qeros ceremonial center at the edge of the jungle, where the Carnival festival was to be held. Each Qeros family has a large house here, used only for community feasts. We were told that people would be drunk and not responsible for their actions, and further that the community authorities were sending us a note from the ceremonial center telling us not to come or to be prepared to pay one million soles in order to film there. Someone said that the people were angry and were gathering stones to use in their slingshots against the filmmakers. Although no note arrived, just minutes before we started our descent down the mountain, the *alcalde* (mayor) and his *rechidor* (assistant) arrived on horseback. They were drunk beyond reason and were singing, and they told us that it had been decided that we should not disturb the festival. The *alcalde* held the responsibility (called a *cargo*) for the affair and didn't want any trouble. I attempted to explain my position to him and revealed the agreement I had made with the president the year before, but he just sang with his eyes closed as I talked, so that I couldn't be heard. Eventually he stated that last year's president had been replaced, and he said I was welcome to be at the festival but that I could not film unless I had the agreement of the community. So on the basis of presenting my case to the Qeros authorities, we went down the mountain, descending four thousand feet in four hours, through pouring rain, and finally entering into the silent and deserted ritual center of Hautun Qeros.

Raymundo, Andrea, and Nicholasa Quispe Chura as children, 1956. John Cohen photographed these same three again in 1977 and in 1983.

Opposite page, above: Raymundo at a ceremony for the strength and fertility of llamas, 1977. The llama is being given chicha *(corn beer).*

Opposite page, below: Raymundo at the hamlet of Wayuna Pampa, high above the ceremonial center of Qeros

Nicholasa and her daughter, 1977

Andrea and her daughter,
1977

Left, above: Andrea and her son, 1983

Left, below: Andrea and her daughter, 1983

Right: Andrea's daughter with her daughter, the baby whose death John Cohen mentions, 1983

The first task was to find a place to stay. We entered, leaving the horses and equipment on the edge of town. Earlier, in the hamlet of Wayuna Pampa, Henrique Samata had invited us to stay in his house in Hautun Qeros, but it was closed and he wasn't there. I suggested that we stay on the edge of town in a building that belonged to the community, but our guide, Jubernal Diaz, thought that would be worse—for in the event that the community did not welcome us, we would be in serious trouble. So we opened Henrique's door and moved our gear inside. An old man who used this house to store potatoes told us we could stay that night but would have to leave if we weren't permitted to film. He said that the Japanese had been thrown out and were not going to be permitted to film at Carnival. People were angry about them. As it grew dark, Qeros families arrived from the paths above. No one spoke to us, and we were suddenly isolated and surrounded in the center of the village. We were hoping for a signal of recognition or welcome, but none was forthcoming. It felt as if we were in some kind of prison, or didn't exist for those around us.

With a flourish, the *alcalde* of Qeros galloped in on his horse. We had last seen him in the mountain hamlet that very morning. Now he was in full costume with bright streamers and Samurai-like dress. He fell off his horse drunk. A boy laughed and the man gave us a mistrustful glance. Everybody seemed irrational and potentially hostile.

All evening we watched shadows pass our door and looked for indications of how we were to be received. We did not know whether it was safe to go out into the crowd. Conch shell trumpets were playing outside our house and we couldn't be certain if we were being threatened or ignored. We watched for new developments while trying to interpret what was happening around us.

Peter became depressed. He feared that our filming would disrupt his relationship with the Qeros. At dark he walked through the village looking for his old *compadres*, and he encountered a woman he had been close to. She ignored him. He became more upset and withdrawn and his gloom af-

fected us all. The guide announced that it would be impossible to prepare dinner that night, for all the streams had been muddied by the horses and people running around the village. There were wild sounds of chanting and shouting all around the house, and no Qeros came to greet us.

We attempted to vent our frustration by cursing the damage the Japanese had done. It seemed clear that their practice of paying in order to film had changed the meaning of culture for the Qeros, turning daily life into a commodity. At the same time they feared these changes, they were also willing to accept the payments. Somebody told us that the Japanese had already paid the million soles and had presented the Qeros with sickles and *trago* (drinking alcohol). We figured this would keep the Qeros drunk, irrational, and greedy in any negotiations.

In the morning I announced that I was abandoning the plan to film and would no longer push for dealing with the authorities. The situation had become too uncertain and seemed potentially dangerous to us. Images of the massacre of the journalists in Ayacucho entered my head, and I could see parallels in the situation. We too were outsiders dealing with an unnamed and undefinable native rationale.

Early that morning, several of Peter's *compadres* came up to greet him. They said that by night they did not recognize him. Groups of Qeros were moving rapidly through the village greeting and visiting each other. The Carnival became a reuniting of the separated villages of the community. I recognized Francisco Flores from the hamlet in the mountains. He winked at me and went right on. I recognized Santos from our filming seven years before. He embraced me and smiled. After all the tension, it was very touching and reassuring. He left with a group of Qeros. An optimism emerged. We said, "Let's be cool and possibly we'll be able to film now, if the feelings come from them."

A man dressed in an Addidas running suit came over and announced in English that we must come see, for the Japanese had arrived. In a field just down the path from our house stood a strange film crew, men in bright yellow synthetic fabric jackets with KODAK FILM printed on them. There were an athletic cameraman who looked prepared to assault a mountain and a tall young man from Lima with a genteel manner looking very chic in clean white pants and a white hat. There were also assorted runners, assistants, guides, and translators. There were too many people here for the small Qeros community. I spoke with the chief of the Japanese film crew. He was a serious, decent person. I said I'd heard about his filming and liked the way he had been following a single family over several years to record social change. I told him also that I had serious differences with the approach of paying everyone for each scene. And I said we had a most delicate situation with the Qeros before us. I suggested that if we did film, we should try to be considerate of each other. The Japanese filmmaker said that they did not pay for their filming and that we had only heard a story that was circulating about them. Further, they had heard from the Qeros that *we* were paying to film. We realized that the Qeros had been playing us off against each other.

Yoshiharu Sekino, the filmmaker, said that he had missed the showing of my Qeros film in Cuzco by one day last year. He said that television had no interest in his Qeros project or in a similar film he was making about the Machiganga tribe in the jungle. Japanese television only liked a film he had done about the making of an Inca bridge. We talked of our similar problems with TV. When I asked him how he funded these projects without TV backing, he laughed. His family and friends were helping him. He was a medical student who got sidetracked into his interest in anthropology and law and had written a thesis on the subject. He hoped to go back to medical school. I told him he must be crazy like me to have become so obsessed with the Qeros. He agreed and told me he had come directly from Japan to film Qeros Carnival and was going right back afterward.

One of the guides told us that the new president of Qeros was sleeping and that we must discuss any arrangements with him as soon as he arrived. We realized that the ceremony was supposed to start within the hour. Shortly, the president came and announced that the Japanese must pay half a million soles and give sickles and alcohol in order to film. I was told that I would not be permitted to film unless I paid one million soles and gave the sickles. Yoshi said to the president—who was an unpleasant and insistent person—that we were going to resolve this payment jointly. The president announced that he would return in half an hour, and that we should have an offer ready. The Japanese and I agreed to pool our resources and to limit the number of people involved in the filming. Then I suggested that we pray to the Apus and the Aukis (Qeros mountain spirits), as well as to Buddha, Jehovah, and Confucius.

While we were talking, one of the guides for the Japanese made a private deal with the Qeros president, offering him a special payment for his cooperation. This would be separate from the community donation. When the president returned to us, he restated his original position. I was kneeling by Yoshi and became very tense as the guides negotiated with the Qeros. Everything seemed settled, and we were asked to wait outside for the final word. While I was preparing the camera, they told us that things were "all set." I began to wonder how the Qeros would be notified, and how they could change their attitude toward us in such a short time. But before any public announcement could be made, the Qeros started to assemble for their Carnival, and the Japanese started filming. I was told by Peter to wait for a public presentation of money and sickles, but when I saw the Japanese running all over the place with their camera, I thought there was a misunderstanding and I prepared to film from my stationary position with the tripod.

*Above: Qeros man arguing
with a mestizo, 1957*

*Opposite page: A Qeros
elder spinning wool to
make yarn*

A strange excitement set in, for the Qeros began to run about, bringing *chicha* (a fermented beverage) and tables to the plaza in front of their church. Conch shell trumpets were blasting, and groups of Qeros with flutes were whizzing by. And the Japanese cameraman kept rushing in front of the Qeros, filming like a pilot on a hit-and-run mission. A Qeros man became annoyed with the cameraman and attacked him with the table he was carrying. A second Japanese interceded while the cameraman ran off to film elsewhere. A line of dancers went by, and I filmed them from above on the hill. There were several still photographers with the Japanese who were set up with telephoto lenses on tripods, and the whole affair was beginning to resemble a media event. A young woman teased me in Quechua, "Are you going to pay me one million soles?" Someone yelled "Watch out for stones!" My hand was on the switch of the camera and I felt a sudden sharp pain in my finger. It went cold and numb, and I could see the bruise at my knuckle. Someone saw the large stone the woman had thrown so accurately at me. Only a half inch difference would have smashed my expensive rented camera. Another rock went by the face of the guide.

The Attack

There was a strange silence as the Japanese filmmaker talked again with the Qeros president. Together we calmly filmed in the plaza at a table full of conch shells where the village authorities sat. I returned to my station on the hill and filmed a passing line of dancers. I saw a man dressed in full Qeros costume, accompanied by an older man, come running up the hill to my side. Suddenly they were confronting me. All I could do was say, "Pardon me if the camera is a disturbance." The older man repeated the word *disculpe* (pardon) and then he struck me in my face and on my arm. I tried to protect the camera and he kicked me. Others joined in hitting me. I didn't want to hit back, only to defend myself from

the blows. The old man struck me on the temple and I started to black out—I barely kept from collapsing and felt absolutely helpless. There were possibly five people hitting me. I could see the Japanese running into the house, also under attack. I was separated from them by a mass of angry people. I looked to the hill above me and could see I was surrounded by Qeros. It was like a scene in a cowboy movie, and I thought of the rocks they might be carrying. Although the idea of starting up the camera came to me, I was too busy trying to defend myself. Peter handed our tape recorder into a house and yelled at me to get back to our place. I lifted the heavy camera and tripod, clambering down stones and into the stream while I was being kicked and punched. I called for Jubernal, our guide, who was in front of me. The Qeros turned on him and pushed him up against a wall and kicked him in the groin, head, and hand. Peter passed by and they started after him. Somehow, we three managed to duck into our place and shut the door. We feared it would be broken in. Shortly, the young wife of Henrique joined us in the house. She was terribly scared as well. Then a heavy rain from the jungle drenched the village, and it became silent.

We remained close to the house all that day and night, afraid to wander out or come close to the Carnival dance, which we could hear but not see. During that day several Qeros came to visit and offer apologies. They reported that the Japanese had left and that our sickles had been taken by the people. Several Qeros appeared bruised and beaten; the pent-up feelings released by intoxicating *chicha* beer resulted as much in fighting and expressions of old resentments as they did in greetings and reunions.

This opening up of deep feelings is the emotional basis of this religious fiesta. Most of the year the Qeros are separated from each other in their isolated villages. They spend many hours alone each day in the high pastures with the flocks of llamas and alpacas. Their coming together at Carnival has many divergent results—one of which is the releasing of tensions. We learned the identity of those Qeros who had attacked us. Most of them were from villages where the Japanese had filmed earlier, and probably these were people who had *not* been filmed and had watched their neighbors across the stream grow rich while they were excluded from the gifts and attention for several years. It certainly gave an explanation for their resentment of filmmakers.

I expressed anger that our sickles had been taken and said that I would report it to the district police if they were not returned. The following morning, the secretary of Qeros came and admitted that he was one of those who had attacked us, and that he felt it wrong that our sickles were taken, so he had gone around and collected them from the takers. But he wouldn't return them to us unless we gave him several for himself. I was disgusted by this type of ransom but was persuaded to acquiesce in the demand so as to avoid getting involved with the regional police.

A Contemplation

We never were sure what had happened. Had we been the focus of deep community resentment, or was it just a few people against us? Were we only a small element in the Carnival uproar? Was our relation to the Qeros wrecked forever, and is the idea of further filming out of the question? What were the key ingredients of the troubles? One clue was given by Faviano Quispe Chura, an old man up in the highlands. He was troubled at the way new ideas were disrupting Qeros traditions, and he didn't like the way that the young people were accepting gifts and payment with no sense of the tradition of reciprocity that governs their lives. He feared that they would grow accustomed to taking payment without working for it or deserving it.

Although I agreed with him, there was nothing I could do about it. My own moral decision to bring gifts to help the entire community as an alternative to individual payments was a failure. There was no way to communicate to the Qeros any possible benefits which might come from my film, although years ago Domingo Samata, then president of Qeros, had announced at a ceremony, "We don't know exactly what this man is doing, but I feel it will be good for us." On the basis of his statement I was allowed to film the ceremony. How could I show the Qeros that my film presented them in a favorable light to the outside world, and why should this matter to them? Traditionally the neighboring villages and the mestizo communities have viewed the Qeros as dirty brutes, the uncivilized *chunchos* of the Andes.

According to anthropologist Steven Webster, who knows the Qeros well, the problem with my film and outlook on the Qeros is that there is too much stress on the importance of survival and not enough attention given to their modernity. The Qeros have demonstrated their ability to construct defenses to deal with the mestizo world, and they have developed the capacity to be devious in dealing with life outside their community. This ability to have a separate face and a different set of standards for a hostile world, while preserving their private traditional beliefs for themselves, has become the strategy that connects the Qeros to most of the "Fourth World" of Third World native peoples.

"Bleows"

The Whaling Complex in Bequia

BY HORACE P. BECK

PHOTOGRAPHS BY JANE BECK

Looking out for whales, 1972

Carleton Mitchell once referred to the island of Bequia in the Lesser Antilles as "a working mariners museum."[1] And so it is. Bequia is the only island in the West Indies where people hunted, and still hunt, the humpback whale in about the same way it was hunted when Melville went a-whaling. Indeed, it is one of only two places in the world where humpbacks are still fished, the other being the Kingdom of Tonga in the South Central Pacific.

This whale-hunting at Bequia has had a singular effect not only upon the island community but also upon the positions Bequians hold throughout the islands. In an area where interisland enmity is rife, Bequia alone is respected and admired throughout the Lesser Antilles. All of this is due to "Old Bill" Wallace, and accordingly a few words are required to set the scene.[2]

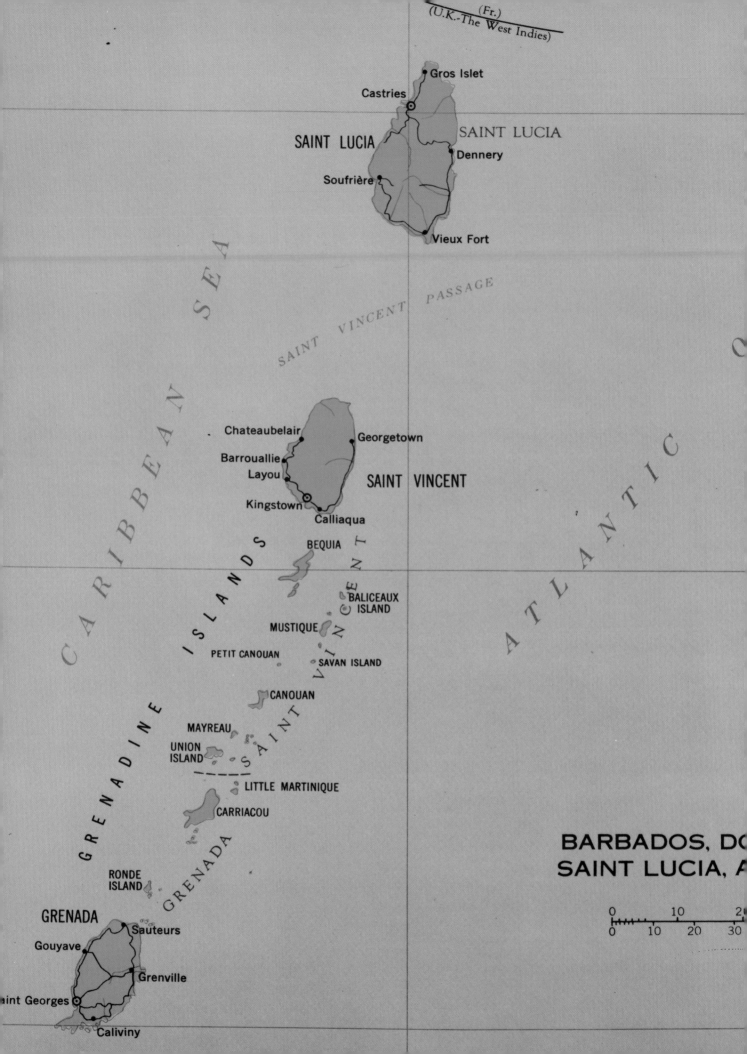

Gros Islet

Castries ⊚

SAINT LUCIA

SAINT LUCIA

Dennery

Soufrière •

Vieux Fort •

SAINT VINCENT PASSAGE

CARIBBEAN SEA

Chateaubelair •

Barrouallie •

Layou •

Kingstown ⊚

Georgetown •

SAINT VINCENT

Calliaqua •

BEQUIA

G R E N A D I N E

I S L A N D S

BALICEAUX
ISLAND

MUSTIQUE •

S A I N T V I N C E N T

PETIT CANOUAN

• SAVAN ISLAND

CANOUAN

MAYREAU

UNION
ISLAND

S A I N T

LITTLE MARTINIQUE

CARRIACOU

G R E N A D A

RONDE
ISLAND

A T L A N T I C

GRENADA

Gouyave •

Sauteurs •

• Grenville

aint Georges ⊚

Caliviny •

BARBADOS, D□

SAINT LUCIA, A

0   10   2□
0   10   20   30

William Wallace (the father of "Old Bill") was born in Strathrea, Scotland, joined the navy, served in the West Indian "Station," and came to Saint Vincent, where he was discharged and became the manager of Friendship Estate in Bequia, which was owned by Thomas Warner. When Friendship Estate went bankrupt Wallace bought it in. He married Elizabeth Brown, the widow of an English army officer, and had two sons by her—Charles, and William Thomas, Jr., who was born in November 1840 on the island of Bequia.

The boys' mother died when Bill was five, and his father then married Sarah Ann Warner, widow of Thomas Warner, original owner of Friendship Estate. The father died, leaving an imperfect will, when the boy was fifteen, and four months later Bill, Jr., bound himself to the Hughes Island Company and on March 15, 1856, went to sea "against my dead father's wishes." He traveled extensively in the merchant marine, suffering seasickness, hurricane, war, smallpox, yellow fever, shipwreck, mutiny, and a few other vicissitudes, all carefully set down in his journal, part of which has been devoured by slicks and still more burned for spite in a family feud.

In 1857 he shipped aboard a Yankee whaleship in Saint Vincent, where apparently he acted as a shantyman, for he "was asked to come aft and play a tune for him [a mate with smallpox] on the violin." His peregrinations took him into several whaleships and carried him to Provincetown, where he met and subsequently married Estella Curran, and to New Bedford, where he learned boat-building.

Eventually he returned to Bequia with his wife, settled down on part of his inherited estate, and started a new enterprise, a shore whale fishery. Meanwhile, he sired a number of offspring both "in" and "outside" the family, until his wife finally took ship for home, remarking that she would prefer going to hell to returning to Bequia, a vow we know she partially kept, for she never came back.

Old Bill, as he came to be known, was faced with a monumental task, and he did it well. He had to teach the locals how to build boats, how to rig them out for whaling, how to look out for whales, how to approach a whale (in those days not only humpbacks but right and sperm whales also), how to harpoon it, fight it, kill it, bring it ashore, butcher it, and process it.

He gave his men a costume—a large floppy hat, wide pantaloons, a knife, a walking stick, and a whaler's pan (a painted lard pail containing a lunch). He gave them a language composed mostly of his big-ship lingo, which sometimes sounded absurd when applied to whaleboats. For example, "Let fly de jib tackle falls!" requires loosing a halter knot in a piece of string. He gave them songs (sea shanties) and taught them how to compose them, and narrative songs as well. He taught them small-boat handling, how to keep station when sailing in company, how to heave to without losing ground while waiting for a whale, how to handle the whaling oars in muffled oarlocks and "spring ahead" in perfect unison at forty-four strokes a minute and "toss oars" at the end, how to sheer the boat with the steering sweep, and how to keep the whale line clear, "wet the line" and coil it, and maintain it. He taught them how to cook whale meat, preserve it, try out the blubber, and clean the bone. In so doing, he instilled in the population a longing for whale meat. Beyond this he established elaborate rules to control the fishery:[3] which boat was entitled to strike first, what obligation other boats had in regard to the "fast" boat, who owned a whale that had broken loose or that had been killed but first broke away, how the profits should be divided—not only among the crew but among all who had a part in the taking of the whale. He delegated responsibilities within the boat—who bailed, "wet de tub," "throw down de spar," and so on—as well as determining rewards for the harpooner, boat steerer, and others. All of this he had learned from tradition, and thus he started a true folk occupation.

The task he set for himself was not easy. After more years than I care to remember I have learned one thing: West Indian blacks are among the most tradition-oriented people I have known. They resist change, in proof of which I would suggest that although they have forgotten some of what Old Bill taught, they have not replaced it with improvisations, nor have they changed a single item. In fact, they refused to use Dacron sails for several years in the 1970s because "Bill Wallace don't use them" and came to them only after their canvas ones were totally destroyed. The only change from Bill's teachings is the use of a walkie-talkie to supplement Old Bill's heliographic communication system, and half the time it fails to work because the batteries are dead, they forget to bring them, or the machines simply "mash theyself up."

How he managed to achieve his goal is hard to say, although there can be no doubt

he did. At one time there were seven "fisheries" on Bequia with four boats, six men each, to a fishery.[4] The occupation has survived for over a hundred years, although in greatly reduced numbers (only two boats still hunt). It survived ten years when no one saw a single whale. It survives despite the fact it never showed a decent profit, and it survives today with less than a whale and a half per year since 1960 and despite all that the ecologists, environmentalists, and busybodies can do to stop it.

What Old Bill did he did for his own profit. That he created a new culture was incidental, though it aided him, undoubtedly, in recruiting and holding good men. The blacks themselves he held in scorn— "those jumbie crabs," he called them to Fritz Fenger in 1912.[5]

Straightening the harpoon, 1975. The whole instrument weighs nearly eighty pounds.

Certain things Bill had on his side that helped immeasurably in implanting a New England folk occupation in the West Indies. Whether it was by accident or through his own discoveries in Africa, Bill made use of many traditional values whose origins lay in Africa as well as more recent, local ones. The first of these was courage. In Africa a greeting is "May you have strength," with the implication not of good health but of superior prowess. To overcome one's adversary physically, to confront danger, to display sexual success all denote the brave man. And to the West Indian the world is full of terrifying possibilities. There was the danger of being killed by the whale and swallowed up by the sea. The men who went whaling arrived at the boats before first light. This meant that many must walk a narrow track in the small hours of the morning when the jumbies (ghosts) were out. For some,

moreover, the track led across Qualm Gutter and Lowby (Low Bay) Gutter, areas well known for their population of assorted supernatural beings.

The African and the West Indian love ritual, and whaling became ritualistic. The boats were launched and whaling begun on February 1, unless that date fell on a Monday, which was an unlucky day. Before the boats pushed off, they were decked in flowers and blessed by a priest, a feast was held that everyone attended, and the boats were sprinkled with rum. The boats pushed out at a set hour each morning and returned at a set hour, with half a day on Saturday and no whaling on Sunday. The boats were ritually hauled ashore on the bones of defunct whales, blocked up by whale vertebrae. The season was finished May 1 and the boats laid up till next year.

Costume is extremely important to West

Indians and to Africans as well. Said Lincoln Simmons of Belmont (Bequia), "Give a West Indian a uniform and an oil barrel for an office and I tell you, man, he think he governor." The clothes, the hat, the knife and pan, along with the staff of authority, all fill this requirement, and it is said that the people living along the track could tell the hour by the tapping of the whaler's stick as he moved to the boats in predawn darkness.

West Indians enjoy brief periods of intense activity interspersed with long periods of tranquillity. They are galvanized into action at a dog-baiting or cockfight, and when it is over they relax, doze, and tell endless stories of previous activities. Whaling affords exactly this kind of action.

Lying under the fig tree on the hill, they peer out over the sea for whales, while they spin yarns and play practical jokes like "putting fire to someone," sticking a horse nettle into somebody's pants, or arranging a fishhook to jig someone when he gets up. A whale is sighted. Everyone shouts orders. They "fly" to their boats and try furiously to get up to the whale. If they succeed, there is a long period of waiting for the whale to rise, the rush to drive home the harpoon, then the wildest activity. The whale line smokes on the loggerhead, the boat groans from the strain, spray slashes over the bows, the whale roars and thrashes the water to foam, and the crew are covered with blood from his spout. The shore is thronged with semihysterical spectators. It's heady stuff,

and there is a long period of leisure to sit in the rum shop and discuss it.

Cutting up and trying out is something else again. It is a bloody but unexciting period of demanding work that sometimes takes more than three days. It is plain hard work, and before many hours the whalers begin to drift away, with the result that sometimes a considerable portion of the whale is lost.

The sea itself has charisma. During slavery only the most trusted slaves were allowed to go out on it, for the less trustworthy might skip off, commit a clumsy act and wreck the boat and gear, or drown themselves. Further, it was a highroad to adventure and freedom. Hence there remains a desire to spend one's time on the roaring sea. It is also believed that the sea will drown evildoers,[6] so that those who venture forth on it must be at least somewhat virtuous.

When a man catches a whale he demonstrates his prowess in several ways. Although it takes a collective effort, the result is usually regarded as a personal success. The whale is the largest creature alive, and for a 150-pound man to kill it in a twenty-six-foot pulling boat clearly entails a display of great strength and courage. To drive the iron home in the first place necessitates being able to outwit leviathan, whose intellect is thought to be in proportion to his bulk. According to an informant, one of the more famous whalers (after Bill Wallace) augmented the reputation he gained from killing whales by sailing from Isle a Ronde to Bequia in the dark with only his cook: "In each channel [there are five] he have intercourse with she."

Finally, Wallace did not have to start quite from scratch. Bequians had been going in small numbers to whale on ships that put into Saint Vincent for water.[7] This gave him a small number with whom to work.

Along with the traits of culture he could work on there were others he could do little about. Although the West Indian admires courage, it may be because that is a rare commodity.[8] In times of stress there is a tendency to panic in the boats. On one occasion when a whale came up beneath the boat there was general consternation, and one man cried out, "Lookee! Lookee! Yonder comes de whale! Blessed Jesus! Oh, it fair melt me bowels!" On another occasion the whale nudged one of the boats, and the harpooner threw his iron over the opposite side. To combat this, Wallace, knowing they loved sayings and fraternities, gave them to understand that they were "brothers together" and "if the whale kill one it mus' kill all." This tactic availed little. Most crews will not hunt sperm whales, considering them too ferocious, and are even reluctant to go on a bull humpback.

A second difficulty Wallace never resolved was that West Indians are neither very inventive nor forehanded. In a hundred years there have been almost no innovations in the whaling trade. If anything breaks or miscarries, there is never anything to repair the damage, nor is there any effort to do so. I once pointed out that the mast of a boat I was in had a crack in it, but nothing was done about it, and four days later it broke about three hundred yards from shore. We returned to the beach, and although there was a usable mast on the shingle, no one was interested in transferring the sails and shrouds. The crew went home.

As I mentioned, West Indians seem to enjoy their place in the sun inordinately. Each man is a "hero," and he would rather achieve nothing than see someone else succeed. There are tales of boats ramming other boats to prevent their taking a whale, of sending boats off on a wild goose chase when they were most needed, for fear the other boat might "get fast first." There is at least one ridiculous account of a boat's throwing a harpoon over another to prevent its getting fast first. An especially good harpooner was believed to have been pushed off a cliff and his neck broken.

Enmity runs high, and revenge is sweeter than success. Harpoon lines are cut, the walkie-talkie sabotaged, the spyglass stolen, the pin pulled out of the harpoon. Lookout stations are declared off limits by their

owner, whose act serves to deprive him of whale meat and cash.

Neither is there much cooperation.[9] When a whale was killed and "went bottom" in 120 feet of water a diver was needed. The best diver was a relative of the harpooner, but he was busy diving for lobsters. Two other divers were then employed; taken to the very spot, they found the whale on the first dive. They passed lines to it and the whalers hauled it up. Although the divers had no prior knowledge of where the carcass was, could not have hauled it up, did not know how to butcher it, had no way to process it and no idea of how to dispose of it, they claimed it for their own. Much of the whale spoiled before the problem was resolved. Speaking of the relative who was lobstering when needed, an informant said, "I tell you mon, that ―――― rather gaze into the two loving eye of a lobstaire than help he best friend."

Perhaps the greatest source of unrest is the pay system. Wallace used the traditional share system universally accepted (and also detested) in Yankee whalers. Under this arrangement, disproportionate amounts or shares are distributed to owners and crews— so much for the boat, so much for the owner, and so down the line. Invariably the crew feels this is unfair. Moreover, since part of their portion is paid in blubber, bone, and meat, some of which is always stolen, and some thought inferior to others' portions, hard words are passed and devious routes followed to assuage the presumed injury. The methods vary from poisoning the harpooner's dog to frightening off the next whale to practicing black magic.

Despite its problems and its lack of financial success, whaling remains the pulse of Bequian life and the reason for the islanders' superior position among the Lesser Antilles. An enormous amount of island culture has permeated the occupation. From many examples, two will suffice—the use of *obeah* and the employment of dreams.

In the past it was common practice to work *obeah* against another fishery to prevent its men from catching whales, and there is a belief that some of the dry periods of whaling were due to that practice. Indeed, it was so common as to work its way into folksongs. For several years I thought it was something out of the past, since my stock question, "Do you have *obeah* here?" was always answered by, "No, no *obeah* in Bequia."

Then one day, after nearly a month with no sightings, one of the whalemen asked me, "Do you believe you can put something in the water to keep cow whale away?"

"I thought there was no *obeah* in Bequia."

"There ain't. We brings it from Saint Vincent."

It seems that a member of the crew felt himself abused and paid money to an *obeah* man in Saint Vincent to drive away the whales he presumably was hunting.

Later on I discovered that *obeah* can help as well as harm whaling. I was asked if I would like to catch a whale, and I assured the person I would.

"You mus' give me $1200, and you kotch de whale."

"How's that?"

"I give it to a fella in Saint Vincent, and he make things like they was."

Dreams in the West Indies are of great importance.[10] Before undertaking any serious enterprise, people seek dream references. If these are auspicious, the venture is deemed worth undertaking; if inauspicious, it is abandoned or held in abeyance until dream assurances are forthcoming. Frequently the undertaking is altered according to dream advice. So popular and important are dream messages that they have been codified. The best or most certain results are in dreams from the dead—friends, relations, and parents, in ascending order. Usually, to dream of one's dead mother or relation who was closest is the most important. However, dreams generally need interpretation, and this, too, is codified. For example, to dream of corn means money; white children bathing in the sea, good luck; sheep feeding on a hill, success. An airplane tells of a trip, but a burning or falling plane means death, a horse means a message, and

*Sighting the flukes in the
distance, 1972*

The chase, 1972

a ship going away from one means disaster. To dream of certain individuals means ill fortune. While all dreams are important, certain people have a reputation for having especially pertinent dreams.

Nearly every whale caught is caught after a dream—and usually much in the fashion described in the dream. There can be little doubt that dreams have an effect upon the crew. For if one has an auspicious dream, the entire temper of the boat will accelerate, whereas if it is bad or nonexistent, there will be an air of indifference and even resistance to the activity. Lest someone think that the dreams are tailored to fit the cloth, they are usually revealed before the event, and I, for one, am convinced that they may well be self-fulfilling in that they have a psychological effect.

Oddly enough, the information within the dream does not ordinarily come from the dead but is instead revealed either through friends of the living or through interpretation of the dream content. One morning my companion told me on the way to the whale boats that we would get a whale that day. Further, he said, we would meet it in the channel between Isle a Côte and Petit Nevis. That is where we met, and that is where we got fast to, a large bull (which subsequently "drew the iron").

Athneal Ollivierre, the head harpooner, dreamed that he was rushed by a large horse (see page 49). He drew his knife and stabbed it twice, and the beast ran off. Athneal interpreted this to mean he would harpoon a whale.

Occasionally dreams need little symbolic interpretation. One night Athneal dreamed that he was taking his cow up the mountain to pasture when "she began to act very cross. I picked up a stick and knock the old bitch down." The calf promptly ran away ("he fly fly from me") downhill and Athneal, busy

with the cow, saw his boat steerer, Joseph Ford, coming toward him and called to Joseph to stop the calf, which he did.

Ollivierre interpreted this dream to mean he would take a cow and a calf whale next day, and so it transpired. The cow whale butted the boat (acted cross) before he lanced her and her calf swam down wind until Joseph Ford put the whale boat in position and it too was taken.

His wife, Hilda—one of those persons with a special reputation for significant dreams—dreamed that Athneal's dead mother brought her "four fowl's eggs." When she awoke she prepared an extra large breakfast for her husband, for, she said, the dream meant he would catch four whales for the season, and since he had already taken two, the next two were at hand. That day he fulfilled her prediction with a cow and a calf. On another occasion she dreamed that she was walking down a road and a

monkey urinated on her out of a tree. This she interpreted as a whale spout—and another whale was taken.

A final example of Hilda's dreaming occurred in 1980. She was worried about a sick relative and slept badly. After Athneal had gone to the boat, she slept and dreamed that the house, yard, and road were full of people "coming and going." Some she did not know. She thought it was a feast, but there was no food. She realized immediately that Athneal was in danger and tried to warn him. Subsequently he became entangled in the whale line and nearly lost his leg and his life.

Much of the whaling complex rubbed off on the native culture. The natives already had communal work songs such as digging songs, and thus shanties were quite acceptable; the shanties in turn picked up native traits and used them.[11] One, "Do Old Moses,"[12] is a pulling song that uses as its theme the treachery of one fishery to another and how to overcome it. Another is based on the *obeah* being practiced between two fisheries:

Obeah SONG

Here come the "Iron Duke"
Here come the "Iron Duke"
Here come the "Iron Duke"
And what become of "Dart?"

"Dart" is gone to town
To buy a tub of line
"Dart" is gone to town
To buy a tub of line.

Oh Oh North side work the witchcraft
And South side keep it down
Between the eighteen brothers,
Jolly whaler men.[13]

While long narrative verse is not popular in the West Indies, there is one long piece still sung that is interesting as a social and historical document. In 1885 Edward Ollivierre was considered to be the best harpooner on Bequia. He was in the fishery known as England. Dixon Durham, harpooner in another fishery, supposedly pushed Ollivierre off a cliff and broke his neck. Shortly thereafter, Durham got fast to a whale in Bequia Channel. She swung her flukes and beheaded Durham without harming anyone else in the boat, indicating that the sea takes its toll of the wicked. (Dixon bears the dubious distinction of being the only Bequian ever killed by a whale.) The song also indicates that at that time there were three boats to a fishery—six men to a boat:

THE PRINCESS HILL SONG

The first cow whale that Old England
    did beach,
The first cow whale dat Old England
    did beach,
Oh, the first cow whale dat Old
    England did beach,
Old Dixon destroy one of Old England
man.

They speak the word an den do what
    dey say,

*Starting to cut out first
blanket piece, 1974*

They speak the word an den do what
   dey say,
And they speak the word an den do
   what dey say,
Old Dixon destroy one of Old England
   man.

Shame, oh shame, you murderin' crew,
Shame, oh shame, all you murderin'
   crew,
Shame, oh shame, all you murderin'
   crew,
What done in the dark gwine show in
   de light.

Friday evening he bid fare a well,
Friday evening he bid farewell,
Friday evening he bid farewell,
And Saturday forenoon six men pick
   him up.
They speak the word an den do what
   dey say,
They speak the word an den do as dey
   say,
They speak the work an den do as dey
   say,
What done in the dark gwine show in
   the light.

All you go way, all you murderin'
   crew,
All you go way, all you murderin'
   crew,
All you go way, all you murderin'
   crew,
What done in the dark, it will show in
   the light.

Seventeen brothers to wear the
   mourning,
Seventeen brothers will wear the
   mourning,
Seventeen brothers to wear the
   mourning,
Old Dixon destroy one of Old England
   man.

Shame, oh shame, you wondering men,
Shame, oh shame, you wondering men,
Shame, oh shame, you wondering men,
What done in the dark, it will show in
   the light.

You leave his wife and his children to
   mourn,
You leave his wife and his children to
   mourn,
Oh, you leave his wife and his children
   to mourn,
And seventeen brothers shall wear the
   mourning.[14]

There are other areas where the whaling
complex can be noticed. It is a large tourist
attraction. The Bequian flag features a whale.

The rum shops are decorated with whaling
pictures; one that features a whale jaw for
a bar is called the Whaleboner. Shops are
full of scrimshaw (not native) and art dealing with the whaling. One year at Carnival
the island's biggest celebration was won by
a float of a miniature whaleboat pursuing
a papier-mâché whale.

A more important area of endeavor is in
boat-building. All small boats on the island
for whatever use are designed on the whaleboat model. Those not used for whaling
will not have the steering oars, the loggerhead, or sheer chocks, but most have the
bow chock that the whale line runs through.
Even a larger yacht built in Bequia for a
world cruise was on whaler lines and named
Plum Belly.

Today the whaling complex is under increasing strain. On the one hand there is
great effort devoted to prevent the hunting
of whales. Although no one else hunts
humpbacks, and only one or two a year are
killed, environmentalists want the occupation stopped. They aver that the whales may
be exterminated, despite the fact that more
are sighted each year. Yachtsmen, in order
to photograph the whaling, get between the
boat and the whale, and themselves try to
harpoon it with a boathook or shoot at it.
Still others try to frighten the whale away.

More serious is the changing economy.
Cash is increasingly important in Bequia,
and much of whaling flourished on a barter
and a status basis. Now men are encouraged to forsake the sea to work in the hotels or in other jobs created by the tourist
trade. It is safer, more comfortable, and more
profitable to drive a taxi or carry tourists'
bags. The status of the whalers' costume
and staff is now achieved through display-
ing a portable radio or 35-mm camera
(usually without film). Were it not for the
fact that most of the whaling needs were
covered by donations from wealthy white
tourists and landowners, the entire enterprise would have to cease.

In recent years whaling on Bequia has

Cutting up on the third
day, 1972. The whale is
too large to haul on shore
and must be cut up in
shallow water.

changed. As far as I have been able to determine, I was the first nonlocal to go a-whaling on a continuous basis; and I experienced great difficulty in getting aboard. My wife was the first to photograph the whalers and their activities consistently. This was the icebreaker. A Spaniard arrived, paid a huge sum to whale for a winter, and insisted on bringing his wife. Instead of leaving at first light, they left after breakfast. Their pay was to stop when they caught a whale; not surprisingly, none were caught that year.

Now tourist information on Bequia describes "authentic whale hunts," and anyone with sufficient money can go out. Anyone can photograph the procedure, but not

without paying a heavy fee. It is more profitable to romp around the ocean looking for whales than to catch them. Moreover, supercargo in a whaleboat is dangerous. According to an old-time whaler, things are greatly altered. No longer do they pull for a whale, but depend upon sail alone, occasionally augmenting it with paddles. No longer, I am told, do they put out two oars to maneuver when "going on." As a result there have been calamities. We were told, for example, that a crewman stood up to enable a female tourist to "get a better snap." Unfortunately he stood in front of the boat steerer, who lost sight of the whale, which slashed with her flukes and "cut the boat from garboard to sheer plank." Improper

Doving whale meat at Petite Nevis, 1972. The meat is minced, spiced, cooked with blubber, and canned for future use.

positioning in the boat, which prevented a clear view from aft, was a significant factor in the near-destruction of the harpooner in the spring of 1980.

Whatever the future of whaling in Bequia, there can be little doubt that it has done much to determine the character of the island—not only as the islanders appear to their neighbors in the Lesser Antilles, but as they see themselves as well. Because they

hunt the largest living animal in the world they are considered to be a very brave people. The whale is known to be "quicker than a sprat in the sea" and is believed to have intelligence commensurate with its bulk. To hunt it successfully, one must be a consummate boat handler and have a greater degree of sagacity than the prey.

Bequians believe these things of themselves and strive to live up to their image.

Tubs of blubber cooling before trying out, 1972

By West Indian standards, they are skilled and courageous seamen. Not only are they engaged in the trading business and in smuggling, but many go on as hands on the ever-increasing number of yachts. They are remarkable swimmers. One man named King, for example, is said to have saved himself by swimming three days to reach shore. Many are skilled divers, hunting conchs and lobsters in depths of over 150 feet. A very large percentage of them gain their living on the sea—fishing, diving, turtling, and so on. And lest we forget, the whaleboat is the model for all their craft, and they are renowned as boat handlers.

Similarly, in a wider perspective, Bequians' homes and boats are cleaner and better kept than those of other islands. There is less crime on the island, and much of what crime there is is believed committed by an increasingly large number of off-islanders. Although hard to prove statistically, they generally appear to comport themselves better than their neighbors.

Last, they appear as a group braver than others. This can best be described through individual anecdotes. When his whaleboat was pulled under, Athneal Ollivierre found himself alone several miles from shore. Looking down, he saw what he assumed was the whale rising for him. Instantly he attacked it with his knife and was relieved to discover it was the whaleboat rising bottom side up. Another man, diving for lobsters, had an enormous shark grab him by the head. He pulled its jaws apart, extricated his head, and attacked the shark. Most West Indians fear "jumbies" and will blanch at the thought, though on Bequia men have been known to stand against them. On one occasion a man went out with a gun at night to discover what was destroying the young goats. There was a full moon, and he was near Lowby Gutter—the perfect time and place and condition for jumbie visitation. He heard a terrible noise and saw something rolling and tumbling down the hillside toward him. "I think," he reported, " 'Mother God! A jumbie for sure.' " He stood his ground, threw up his gun, and fired, killing the "jumbie" completely. It turned out to be a "ram cat" locked in mortal combat with a young goat.

Whaling has survived on Bequia over one hundred years. It is now in a difficult stage. Over all those years, it has been a cogent factor in the culture—one that Bequians and people from outside the island see as beneficial. One cannot help wondering what will happen on the island if whaling ceases. It is difficult to believe that, by western standards, the consequence will be beneficial.

NOTES

1. Carleton Mitchell, *Isles of the Caribbees* (Washington: National Geographic Society, 1966), 33.

2. The information about Wallace is based on "Old Bill's" handwritten journal, the remnants of which are kept by Miss Olive Wallace, Friendship, Bequia.

3. John E. Adams, "Historical Geography of Whaling in Bequia Island, West Indies," *Caribbean Studies* 11 (October 1971): 64–66.

4. Ibid., 62. Adams cites six stations but overlooks one at Ile-de-Caille.

5. Frederic A. Fenger, *Alone in the Caribbean: The Cruise of the "Yakahoo" in the Lesser Antilles* (London: Hodder and Stoughton, 1917), 106.

6. Jane C. Beck, "Study of the West Indian Devil," unpublished manuscript.

7. Karl Brandt, *Whale Oil and Economic Resources* (Stanford, Calif.: Stanford University Press, 1940), 54.

8. Fenger, *Alone in the Caribbean*, 43.

9. Joel C. Arnoff, "The Interrelationship of Psychological and Cultural Systems: A Case Study" (Ph.D. diss., Brandeis University, 1965), 194–96.

10. Jane C. Beck, "Dream Messages from the Dead," *Journal of the Folklore Institute* 10 (1973): 173–86.

11. See Roger D. Abrahams, *Deep the Water, Shallow the Shore: Three Essays on Shantying in the West Indies* (Austin: University of Texas Press, 1974).

12. Horace P. Beck, *Folklore and the Sea* (Middletown, Conn.: Wesleyan University Press, 1973), 156–57.

13. Sung by Ocarol Ollivierre, La Pompe, Bequia, March 11, 1972.

14. Recorded by Jane C. Beck in the rum shop owned by Walter Bynoe at Paget Farm, Bequia. The informant was Joseph Ford, age seventy-three years.

The *Kalevala*

150 Years, 1835–1985

An Introduction

BY ELENA BRADUNAS

T hose who enjoyed the film *Star Wars* would probably fall under the spell of the Finnish epic *Kalevala*. Though first published 150 years ago, many of the adventures in the epic could easily be scripted into scenes for our modern fantasy adventure films. Instead of battling with advanced technological gadgets such as rockets and laser beams, however, the heroes of the *Kalevala* engage in bouts with words of wisdom and magic runes that cast spells of enchantment over their foes. Thus, when wise old Väinämöinen, the greatest singer of runes, is challenged by a young upstart Joukahainen, it takes but a few magical charms to bury the young man neck-deep in the ground. The frightened Joukahainen

Overleaf: Kullervon goes to war. Fresco by Akseli Gallén-Kallela, 1901. Courtesy of the Embassy of Finland, Washington, D.C.

Reprinted from *Folklife Center News* (October–December), 1984

offers his sister Aino as ransom for his release, and Väinämöinen accepts. The young girl, dismayed by the prospect of marrying such an old man, drowns herself and becomes a fish. Väinämöinen later catches the fish, but does not recognize her and she escapes, leaving him grieving.

Though Väinämöinen suffers setbacks now and then, as a skilled musician and wise charm-singer he is the central figure of the *Kalevala*. Other heroes are either his friends or foes. One adventure follows another, filled with marvelous and fantastic feats. For example, the smith Ilmarinen, who wins the girl of the Northland whom Väinämöinen had set out to court, remains his steadfast friend. Together they go to seek the release of the sun and moon, which Louhi, the evil mistress of the Northland, has sung into hiding. Another memorable episode recounts how Lemminkäinen, the handsome and restless playboy of the epic, is killed while trying to fulfill tasks to win a maiden; his body is chopped into pieces by Death's son. Raking the pieces of the body from the black river of Death's domain, his mother is able to sing life back into him through her knowledge of charms.

These fantastic adventures of charm-chanting heroes and sorcerers were known to illiterate Finnish singers for many hundreds of years. The episodes were sung as individual songs by traditional singers who lived in isolated villages along the Finnish-Russian borderlands. They became known to educated, urban Finns only after the texts of some songs were set down on paper. Although a few of these songs had been sporadically recorded since the eighteenth century, it was primarily the work of one individual—Elias Lönnrot—that clearly demonstrated the richness of these oral traditions. A medical doctor by profession, but an avid folklore collector by avocation, Lönnrot logged many miles on foot in the early 1830s, writing down as many variants as he could find of the songs about Väinämöinen, Lemminkäinen, Ilmarinen, and others. Instead of publishing the songs as individual pieces, however, he arranged them into a linear storyline. In 1835 he published the *Kalevala* as an epic—the Finnish counterpart to the Nordic *Edda*, Germanic *Nibelungenlied,* Scottish Ossian poems, and, harking back to the classics, the Greek *Iliad* and *Odyssey.*

For Finland the publication of songs sung by the ordinary folk in the hinterlands of their country served as a major stimulus to the building and fostering of a distinct national identity. Until then the Finnish language and identity were held in rather low esteem; Finland's educated, urban elite had accepted, for the most part, the language, culture, and traditions of the governing Swedes. Through Lönnrot's *Kalevala* the intelligentsia began to awaken to the richness of the Finnish heritage.

Although it took some time, the *Kalevala* actually helped to kindle national aspirations that eventually led to the establishment of an independent Finland. For the Finnish people, much under the sway of the general romantic trends of the times, the *Kalevala* presented a past of which they could be proud. Scholars argued about the historicity of the heroes, and engaged in discussion about the evolution or devolution of the songs through time. It became required reading in secondary schools, and playwrights, composers, and other artists were soon using its themes and motifs for their own creative ventures.

The *Kalevala* was indeed something of which to be proud, for soon after its publication in Finnish it was translated into Swedish, French, German, and Russian, as well as into Estonian and Hungarian—the two non-Indo-European languages related to Finnish. In America the work generated considerable publicity when Longfellow published his *Song of Hiawatha* in 1885 and critics accused him of plagiarizing the Finnish epic. Longfellow admitted that he was acquainted with the work through German translations and that he purposely copied the trochaic meter of the *Kalevala* in order to imbue his work with a certain ancient and noble tone and cadence. Prompted by the controversy, the English translation appeared in 1889. Since those times translations have been printed and reprinted in thirty languages. The *Kalevala* is probably the best known Finnish literary work throughout the world.

Any folklorist who has studied the history of the folklore discipline will recognize the names of both the epic and the compiler. The recognition comes about because Lönnrot's work inspired other scholars to develop a particular methodology for the study of folklore which for many years influenced the development of the folklore discipline: the comparative historic-geographic method or, referring directly to its origins, the Finnish Method. Julius Krohn, born the year the *Kalevala* was published, is credited as one of the first to articulate the principles which later served as guidelines for the comparative historic-geographic method. Realizing that Lönnrot's unpublished collection consisted of many variants of the same song recorded in different locations, Krohn wondered about the origins and eventual spread of the songs, feeling that some answers to those questions could result from a comparison of text variations from different locales. He was much caught up in the nineteenth century's intellectual fascination with Darwin's evolutionary theory, which underscored the value of empirical studies of variants. After his early death, his son Kaarle Krohn further developed the method, which served as the basis of early folklore scholarship in both Europe and America. Kaarle Krohn became the first professor of Finnish and comparative folklore at Helsinki University, founded the network of International Folklore Fellows, and started publishing the famed FF Communications series, which continues to the present.

Although the comparative historic-geographic method and its underlying premises are not so widely employed within folklore scholarship today, its development played a major role in establishing the study of folklore on a solid academic footing. The method also laid the foundation for the organization of many folklore archives around the world and led to the publication of classificatory indexes such as Stith Thompson's *Motif-Index of Folk-Literature* and *The Types of the Folktale* by Antti Aarne and Stith Thompson. For this reason references to Lönnrot, the *Kalevala,* the Krohns, and the Finnish comparative historic-geographic method will always be part of academic training in folklore.

The *Kalevala* Process

BY LAURI HONKO

n May 1630, two hundred years before the publication of the *Kalevala*, Gustav II Adolf, King of Sweden, issued the first directions for collecting Finnish and Swedish folk poetry. His decree contained detailed instructions on the collection of ancient relics and was preceded by a directive to record "all sorts of chronicles and narratives, ancient tales and poems about dragons, dwarfs, and giants, as well as stories about famous people, old monasteries, castles, the dwellings of kings and cities, from which it will be possible to ascertain how things were in ancient times; old poems about heroes and magic songs, not forgetting to take down their melodies." The preface to the decree reveals that the motive for wanting to collect folk poetry was to demonstrate "that our forefathers were not barbarians," "that we are the oldest nation," and "that our

The Grand Duchy of Finland, showing the region as it was divided into provinces. Elias Lönnrot collected many of his poems in the province of Karelia in eastern Finland. F. De Witt, about 1670. Geography and Map Division, Library of Congress

language is the oldest of all," and it expressed too some concern at the Danish attempt to steal these prizes. With the help of the folk tradition, it was believed, light might be cast upon the way of life of ancient times, the means of livelihood, the history of habitation, the succession of rulers, and the pagan religion.

But Gustav II Adolf's decree should not be taken as an expression of interest in folklore as a living tradition. It was principally a reaction to a similar note sent to the bishops of Norway and Denmark in 1622 by Denmark's Kristian IV. Behind both lay the need to strengthen national identity and to create a favorable view in any comparison of the nations. The discovery of tradition is usually followed by its adaptation for use as an instrument of cultural policy, and the administrative or cultural elite that set the collection of tradition in motion that resulted in the *Kalevala* also bears the responsibility for its new use in an environment quite unlike the one in which it existed before its discovery.

The *Kalevala* is not simply an individual work; it is also a continuing process. In a broad sense this *Kalevala* process can mean the development that began at the time of Henrik Porthan at the end of the eighteenth century, continues today, and will stretch into the future for as long as the *Kalevala* is read. The meaning of this process can be seen in the interpretation of epic folk poetry and of the *Kalevala* at different times—either as the account of historical events or as myth. These two interpretations perform an elaborate balancing act. The historical interpretation has weight whenever it is felt that the national identity is threatened and needs strengthening. The mythical interpretation, on the other hand, gains in importance when internal conflicts and outside pressures are not very strong. Sometimes both interpretations are current simultaneously; but in this case the theory that does not fit with the spirit of the time is pushed aside.

These opposing interpretations may be observed, for instance, in the eighteenth century. They were represented on the one hand by a well-known defender of the Finnish nation, Professor (and later Bishop) Daniel Juslenius and, on the other, by the father of the study of Finnish history, Henrik Gabriel Porthan. The idealistic and patriotic Juslenius had a patchy knowledge of folk poetry, but this did not stop him from making free use of imagination and the historical interpretation of the folk tradition to increase Finland's fame and self-confidence. The cautious and critical Porthan, on the other hand, collected from a number of diverse sources a wide variety of folk poems, realized that they could give an insight into the life and way of thinking of the Finnish-speaking people, and encouraged his students to study Finnish mythology.

The starting point of the *Kalevala* process was Porthan's *Dissertatio de poesi fennica,* published 1766–78. In this work he argued that folk poetry in Finland was highly developed and should even be placed above the poetry to be found in literature. There is a foreshadowing of the direction later taken by folklore research when Porthan says, "Experience has taught me that, by comparing a number of records of folk poems, it is possible to restore them to a more complete and suitable form." Porthan also demanded that folk poems be published without alteration, and that the place and time of collection be recorded.

The importance of Porthan lies in the fact that he endowed Finnish folklore with a new prestige, and that he laid the foundations for folklore research. Porthan was a disciple of the Enlightenment, not of Romanticism; he was producing his works at the time of Johann Gottfried von Herder (1744–1803), but independently of him, for there was in his day discussion at Turku University of Macpherson's Ossian* but not

*Editors' note: In the 1760s James Macpherson published what were purported to be translations of a Gaelic poet called Ossian that were admired for their Romantic spirit. Their authenticity was challenged, however, notably by Dr. Johnson, and a committee appointed after Macpherson's death in 1796 reported that Macpherson had liberally edited traditional Gaelic poems and inserted passages of his own.

of Herder. And in Turku the attitude toward Macpherson remained positive even when Ossian had almost disappeared under the waves of criticism. Porthan and his students compared Macpherson's situation to their own: it was likely, they thought, that his work was based on genuine folk poetry, just as theirs was. They did not, however, come any closer to the idea of an epic proper.

In the Peace of Hamina (1809) Finland ceased to be part of Sweden and came under the jurisdiction of Russia as an autonomous Grand Duchy. The intelligentsia found themselves forced to break off their close cultural relations with Sweden, and the process of their assimilation into Swedish culture, which was already well-nigh complete, came to a halt. On the other hand, they had no affinity with Russian culture. The solution to the identity crisis that ensued was identification with the large majority of Finland's population, the Finnish-speaking but unlettered common people, and in a few decades Finnish, not Swedish, began to gain a position as the common language of the intelligentsia. But the attempt to create a national culture that would satisfy European criteria came up against a triple stumbling block: the language was not adequate for modern needs, the history of Finland was unwritten, and there was almost no literature in Finnish.

It was at this time that Romanticism asserted itself: it painted a new vision of a nation whose common people were not, after all, passive, subjugated, clumsy, and ungifted, but the inheritors of magnificent powers of the mind and spirit that had gone unnoticed until now. The soul and special quality of the Finnish nation was hidden in the oral tradition that had been preserved by the common people. A program for the construction of a national culture began to take shape in the 1810s in the minds of a group of young students at Turku University. A kind of social demand for a national epic was in the air. One of the students, C. A. Gottlund, put forward the idea that

the old Finnish poems might give birth to a new Homer, Ossian, or *Nibelungenlied*, and that the resulting epic would secure the admiration of both contemporaries and posterity for the Finnish nation.

The man who met the demand for a national epic was Elias Lönnrot. Lönnrot believed in the historical interpretation of folk poetry. He was guided in this by his teacher, Reinhold von Becker, who was the first to begin to piece together the story of Väinämöinen from different folk poems in which he appears and to distill from them what von Becker believed to be objective historical facts. Another important inspiration was the Romantic tradition, according to which folk poetry was the nation's historical archive. But Elias Lönnrot was no ordinary collector of folk poems, content to record his material just for the archives. From the very beginning, his work had a conscious aim: publication. It was to this end that he collected folk poems, and once the *Kalevala* was published Lönnrot lost interest in collecting folk poetry.

Elias Lönnrot played his part in the *Kalevala* process between 1828 and 1849. After that, he concerned himself with the *Kalevala* only once more, when he produced an abridged version for schools that appeared in 1862. His active period divides itself naturally into phases according to how he dealt with the original material he collected. Between 1829 and 1831 he published a series of *Kantele* anthologies containing unconnected poems. But even then, Lönnrot allowed himself a freer hand in editing them than had Porthan or Zacharias Topelius the elder, who was to publish his own anthology of folk poetry at the same time as Lönnrot. In his foreword, it is true, Lönnrot gives details of where the poems were recorded; but the published poems are the result of combining different variants and of patching one poem with lines from another. Only three poems appear in exactly the form in which they were recorded.

In the next phase, Lönnrot allowed himself to take greater liberties and combined, for instance, poems about the same character or event. The folk singers from whom he collected the original poems were, certainly, in the habit of combining separate

poems in their local, individual repertoire. The cycles of poems put together by Lönnrot, however, had no such link with any particular area or tradition; they were created from verses collected in many often widely scattered regions.

The next stage was the Proto-Kalevala, in which poems about different characters were fitted into an overall plot. The forging and the stealing of the Sampo, a miraculous object bringing material prosperity, were separated from one another, and in between Lönnrot placed the wooing contest, the wedding at Pohjola, and the still rather disjointed Lemminkäinen and Kullervo ep-

isodes. The basic conflict of the epic—the competition and battle between the people of Kalevala and the people of Pohjola—begins to emerge when the mistress of Pohjola and her beautiful daughter are made the antithesis of the Kalevala heroes led by Väinämöinen.

In creating the structure of the *Kalevala*, Lönnrot sought help from both the folk singers from whom he collected the poems and from contemporary research into the origins of the Finns. In addition, he was encouraged by the so-called Homeric model, the theory that epics are born through a process of combining and editing oral poetry. Lönnrot's experiences on his field trips were decisive: some singers had performed concerted pieces much longer than usual, so unified that they could almost be regarded as miniature epics in themselves, and had also spoken to him of the order in which they supposed the events in different poems to have taken place. In the end Lönnrot was guided by an impression, half of his own invention and half based on learned opinion, of the time when the events of the poems had been a natural part of the life of the ancient Finns. He believed that the religion of these ancient Finns had exhibited many of the characteristics of monotheism, even if the fields and woods were still inhabited by their gods and tutelary spirits, and the respect in which historical figures were held had often led later generations to endow them with godly traits and attributes. This had happened in the cases of Väinämöinen and Ilmarinen. Seeking a place and a time for his visions, Lönnrot put the events in the poems at around a thousand years before, to the south of the White Sea, the area from which the Finns were supposed to have moved into Finland. In moulding this quasi-history, part scientific, part poetic, Lönnrot immersed himself in the world of the *Kalevala* so completely that it began to live a life of its own. It was a question of the ancient history of the Finns and an ancient society of which the *Kalevala* was supposed to be proof.

Although Lönnrot often makes his own role in the creation of the *Kalevala* appear smaller—and the historical and ethnographical value of the work as source material greater—than is actually the case, it is also true to say that he was always ready to speak quite openly about how he had gone about putting together the *Kalevala*.

From the point of view of the comparative study of epics, the question of the authenticity of the *Kalevala* is an interesting one: what resemblance does the epic bear to the folk poems that have been preserved in the oral tradition? What were Lönnrot's intentions as compiler of the *Kalevala*, and how did he use the material he had collected to achieve them?

The attempts of the folk singers themselves to link together poems about the same character created a number of miniature epics that could be called folk epics, none of them more than a thousand lines long. There is no reason to believe that the situation should have been different in previous centuries—that the poems should then have been sung in a more complete form. The structure and form of the *Kalevala* as we know it is Lönnrot's answer to the question that occupied him throughout the time he spent collecting his material: What was the order of the events of which the poems told? And this answer is not a reconstruction, but the creation of Lönnrot's own imagination.

All the same, the number of lines actually composed by Lönnrot is very small—according to one estimate, only about 3 percent. Thus, if the criterion is the authenticity of individual lines, the *Kalevala* is without doubt a genuine folk poetry epic. But of the remaining lines, only a third are identical with Lönnrot's original records. He made alterations in the orthography, language, or poetic meter of about half the lines in the *Kalevala;* from the beginning, he believed that dialect words and phrases and other inconsistencies were unacceptable and could not be allowed to disturb the reader: the work was intended for the entire nation, not for a select circle of scholars. The remaining 14 percent cannot be interpreted as variations of single lines from Lönnrot's original records: they are derived by combining two or more lines.

Thus it is clear that, although Lönnrot did not allow himself a poet's freedom in composing individual lines, he did avail himself of it in compiling the poems—in creating the plot of the *Kalevala*. The *Kalevala* contains very few substantial passages that are word-for-word the same as the originals. Lönnrot combined different vari-

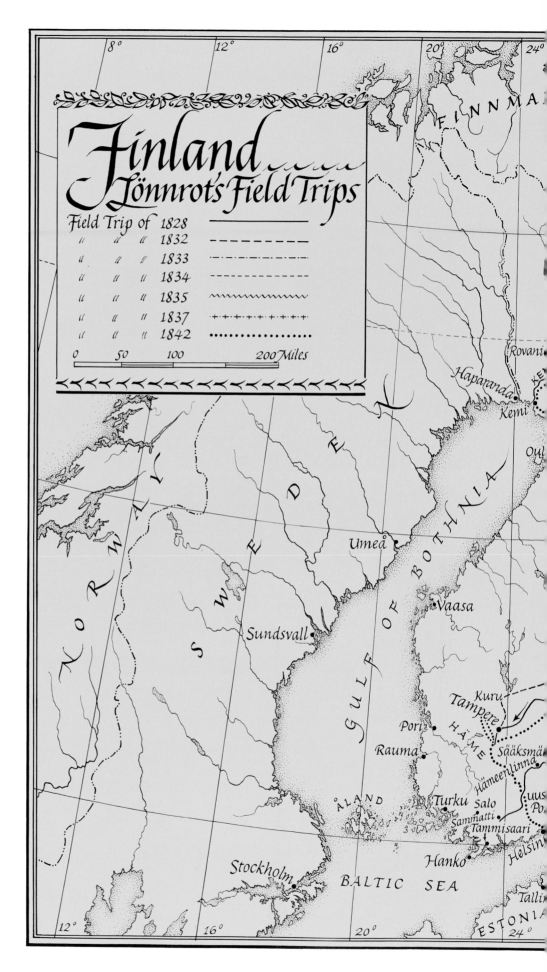

Lönnrot's field trips through Finland. Map by Samuel H. Bryant. Reprinted by permission of the publishers from The Kalevala or Poems of the Kalevala District, *Elias Lönnrot, comp., Francis P. Magoun, Jr., tr. (Cambridge, Mass.: Harvard University Press, 1963). Copyright © 1963 by the President and Fellows of Harvard College.*

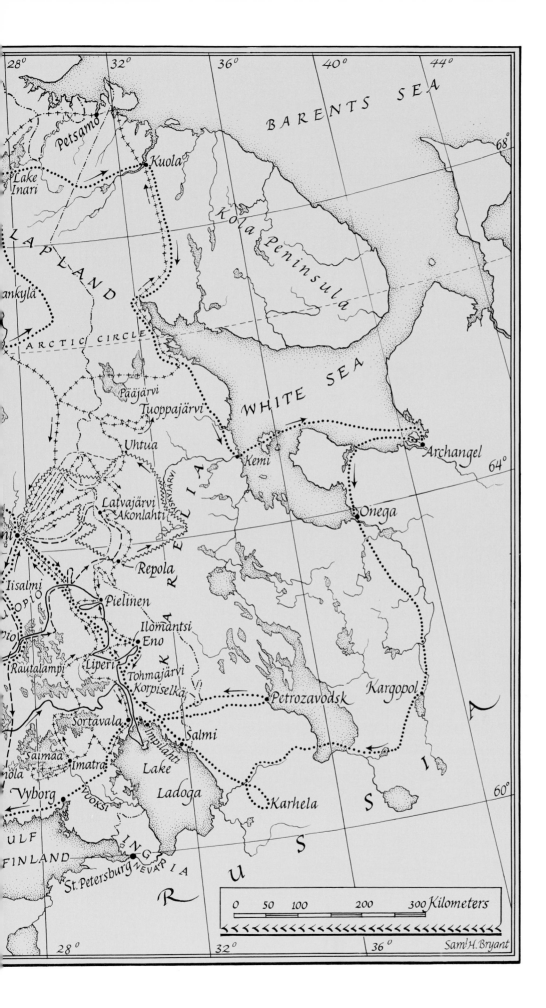

28°   32°   36°   40°   44°

BARENTS   SEA

Petsamo   68°
Kuola

Lake
Inari   Kola Peninsula

LAPLAND

ankylä   ARCTIC CIRCLE

WHITE   SEA

Pääjärvi
Tuoppajärvi   Archangel
                              Kemi   64°

Uhtua

Latvajärvi   Onega
Akonlahti

ni   Repola

Iisalmi   Kargopol

OPIO   Pielinen

io   Ilomantsi
            Eno   S   S
Rautalampi   Liperi
                Tohmajärvi
                Korpiselkä   Petrozavodsk   I
nola   Sortavala
            Impilahti Salmi   A
Saimaa   Imatra   Lake
nola   Ladoga   60°
Vyborg   Karhela

ULF
FINLAND
St.Petersburg   NEVA   INGRIA

R   0   50 100   200   300 Kilometers

28°   32°   36°   Sam!H.Bryant

ants and added parallel lines. The result is that many of the lines appear in context quite different from those of the original oral tradition. At the same time the poems have lost their connections with particular regions, as Lönnrot has no scruples in juxtaposing lines that he had gathered in quite different places. By using this technique Lönnrot was able to create an epic that belonged not to a particular area or province but to Finland as a whole. But it also means that, considered on the level of extended passages, the *Kalevala* is a great deal less authentic than a study of individual lines would suggest.

It was in constructing the *Kalevala's* plot that Lönnrot allowed himself his greatest liberties. On this basis it is reasonable to call him an epic poet—from disparate elements he created a working whole. But his treatment of the plot was made to serve a different purpose that was, artistically speaking, more controversial. For Lönnrot wanted the *Kalevala* to represent the whole range of folk poetry, and consequently he developed a technique of enlargement that allowed him to expand poems at will. He compared variants of the same poem and put together the best lines from each—and as a rule the result was a poem that was far longer than any of its variants. In elaborating the plot his most often used technique was to interrupt the main story with minor episodes. This meant that the narrative moved in a series of stops and starts and that the preparations for an event were apt to swell to quite unjustifiable proportions. This feature was especially obvious in the fifth phase, in the second edition, which appeared in 1849. One of the characteristics of Lönnrot's development was a gradual liberation from the Romantic theory of epic and the adoption of a more consciously literary approach to the *Kalevala*.

Even though not everyone agreed with Lönnrot's theory that the *Kalevala* was an account of the ancient history of the Finns—Jacob Grimm, for instance, believed it should be interpreted as myth—it became dominant to the extent that it was even the official version taught in schools. It was not until the discipline of the study of folk poetry founded in the 1870s by Julius Krohn shifted attention from the *Kalevala* itself to the original folk poems that the mythical interpretation became current once more. The new discipline brought with it the geographical-historical method that was soon applied to the comparative study of folk tales of different cultures. International parallels began to emerge for more and more of the subjects and traditions that had hitherto been regarded as peculiar to one particular area. In this light national traditions began to be seen as common to many nations.

This promising development toward a balanced view of Finnish folk poetry in its international context was cut short by the First World War. And even before it, the Finnish identity had undergone a crisis that disturbed even the peace of scholars. In 1910 a number of newspaper articles criticized the approach of Julius Krohn's son Kaarle Krohn and his followers, accusing them of belittling the value of the *Kalevala* and of seeking in folk poetry evidence of the influence of late medieval Christianity when they should have been dazzled by the ancient and pagan, free and warlike age of the heroes. Four years later Kaarle Krohn announced that his view of Finnish folk poetry had undergone a radical change: contrary to what he had thought until now, the poems contained historical reminiscences of pre-Christian Finland and the heroes whom its inhabitants honored. Abandoning most of his earlier theories, Krohn engaged in a new historical interpretation and later allied himself with Jalmari Jaakkola, the leading authority on Finland's early history. Together these men dominated the scholarly atmosphere between the wars, in which the *Kalevala* poems were regarded as heroic works composed during the Finnish Viking age. This was the climate of thought in which the next generation of scholars was to grow up. The mythical interpretation found only one strong advocate in E. N. Setälä.

After the Second World War fresh winds

Lemminkäinen is rescued from Tuonela, the river of the dead, by his mother (poem 15). Tempera by Akseli Gallén-Kallela, 1897. Courtesy of the Embassy of Finland, Washington, D.C.

Pursued by Väinämöinen, Aino drowns in a lake (poem 4). Aino triptych, oil, by Akseli Gallén-Kallela, 1891. Courtesy of the Embassy of Finland, Washington, D.C.

brought in new methodologies and subjects of interest. Symptomatic of the new attitudes was Martti Haavio's *Väinämöinen* (1950; English translation 1952). The first chapter deals with earlier studies of Väinämöinen; the question posed in the title of the first chapter, "God or man?," receives such a profound and comprehensive answer that the reader leaves it with a clear understanding of the impossibility of a simple answer. The poems tell of at least two Väinämöinens, the shaman and the culture hero; upon these the religious beliefs of the ancient Finns and international myths are deposited layer upon layer. It is no longer possible to make out any putative historical center to the poems, for instance an ancient shaman-seer. But what comes across strongly is an impression of the mythical world-picture of a certain cultural period.

Some recent works have shown that the *Kalevala* process continues today. The historian Matti Klinge's 1983 book *Muinaisuutemme merivallat (Sea Powers of Our Ancient Past)* revives the old controversy. Klinge propagates historical interpretation and western origins for ancient epic poetry. The study is not entirely free from methodological errors, and in the perspective sketched above it is perhaps little more than an anachronism. The author himself admits that he was inspired to write the book by desire to join the battle between eastern and western Finland for the "ownership" of the ancient epic. Consequently the work's true concern is perhaps with what might be called the Finnish soul or identity rather than with the poetry itself. Another historian, Heikki Kirkinen, joins the fray on the other side with rather more carefully chosen arguments. He presents Karelia as an independent eastern cultural area whose influence extended far into western provinces. On this theory, western Finnish characteristics found in the Karelian tradition would be derived from early Proto-Finnic rather than medieval contacts. Kirkinen rejects completely the possibility of interpreting the folk poems historically.

Clearly it is the mythical interpretation of the *Kalevala* that is dominant at present. Lönnrot's theory that the *Kalevala* was at least a signpost to the early history of the

Finns has collapsed. It is no more than a pleasant way of passing the time to attempt to link Väinämöinen, Ilmarinen, Lemminkäinen, or Joukahainen with known historical characters, or even to some exact time or place, or to imagine that all of them existed at some particular time. The layers that folk tradition has added to these figures over the centuries, and to some extent the regional differences in their development, make such a reconstruction impossible in a rigorously scholarly sense. The part played by poems that are undoubtedly historical, such as "The Death of Elina" or "The Poem of Duke Charles," in Finnish epic poetry as a whole is fairly negligible.

The question of the *Kalevala's* ethnographic trustworthiness is a little more complex. The problem is whether the customs and manners, tools and materials, means of transport and weapons that appear in the *Kalevala* bear any relation to the folk culture of any particular area or time. It is certainly true that the objects and customs mentioned in the *Kalevala* have to some extent had their counterparts in living folk culture; in other words, they are not all fictive or poetic. But there are two major obstacles to the wholehearted acceptance of the *Kalevala* as a reliable source of ethnographical information.

The first concerns Lönnrot's method of working, which has already been described. It resulted in a patchwork of colorful pieces, any one of which might for a moment reflect an aspect of a folk culture that actually existed at some time; but even slightly more extended pieces cannot be regarded as trustworthy.

Secondly, it must be remembered that it is by no means certain that even the original poems give a completely faithful impression of the folk culture in which they were born. Between the reality experienced by the singer and the reality of the poems there was always a distance, and to gauge that distance demands both a knowledge of the singer's actual culture and a critical evaluation of the sources using the technique of genre analysis. For instance, bear hunting was always carried out in reality with fire weapons, but in the poems bears are always killed with arrows and spears. Clearly, for Lönnrot, the poems told of an earlier reality; and it was this realization that inspired him to build his fictive ancient Finnish way of life.

To gain a firm grip on the difference between the historical and mythical interpretations it is worth looking at the concept of time. Historical time is linear, continuous, and irreversible, whereas mythical time is cyclical and repetitive; it is born of the union of two different dimensions of time, the magnificent, mythical beginning of the world and the present. Myth is defined as the account of the great beginning (the creation of the world, the decisive start of time), the fundamental events and the exemplary acts of the gods, saints, culture heroes, founders of clans, and so on, based on a common religious world view. As a result of these deeds the world, nature, culture and society, and everything that goes on in them were born and received the order that still exists at present. Thus myth is the justification of the world order: on it are based customs, social institutions, moral rules and norms, the efficacy of religious rites, and the sacredness of cults. History is, in other words, secular time, which myth destroys and replaces with sacred time.

Myths are more persistent than their original ritual contexts, and associated modes of thought, too, can last for a long time even in the absence of real religious activity. From this point of view the concept of myth gives the reader of the *Kalevala* as well as of folk poems some important keys. Many of the stories and their details become easier to understand if we do not try to force them onto the level of historical time and everyday experience but listen to the voice of myth as it speaks to the man who lives in mythical time.

That method of listening starts from the acceptance of folk poems as they are. For instance, it is not necessary to carry out textual criticism, compare variants, or seek distant parallels of a genuine folk poem. The starting point is that in its own context of performance and use it was meaningful and belonged to a complete and living world picture. If there is enough information about that context, the poem can reach us over boundaries of culture and language.

What of the *Kalevala*? Is it possible to approach it in the same way? The answer is undoubtedly yes. The myths of the *Kalevala* are, of course, Lönnrot's variants, but through them it is possible to reach the basic structure of the myth—and that is enough. The message of these ancient myths reaches us through both the *Kalevala* and folk poems. A certain basic structural meaning, that we are not perhaps always able to put into words, remains constant from culture to culture, and it is with reference to this that we understand the meaning of the particular poem at hand and create our own variant of its significance. The abundance of variants is an essential part of the life of myth. Myth is passed on through a series of encounters between performer or source and audience. In giving and receiving myth, both performer and audience create their own interpretation, their own new variant. There can be no grounds, therefore, for rejecting Lönnrot's *Kalevala* because it is "inauthentic"—it is, on the contrary, an authentic follower in the tradition of creative variants from which myth receives its life.

The question of the messages of the *Kalevala* and folk poems is thus tied to the present moment, our ability to receive it, our problems, our fears, and our hopes. But it is important to note that this process of giving meaning is constantly structured by the old myths, many of which also found their way into the *Kalevala*. Scholars, too, may in their interpretations adhere to some mythical motif. Behind the historical interpretations of the *Kalevala* there seems to lurk the myth of a Golden Age, and what is more, in two variants. Romantic scholars applied this myth to the birth of the epic in speaking of a special heroic era without which the epic cannot exist. They have followers in our own age. The competitive interpretation is the Marxist view of the pre-feudal, classless society manifest in the *Kalevala* and folklore, the basic unit being the family or tribal community based on common ownership. The conflict between these two interpretations has had far-reaching consequences in folkloristics and *Kalevala* research. Fundamentally the difference in interpretations is concerned with the nature of the society producing the poems. In both interpretations the trend is toward a state of wretchedness: the Golden Age society vanished, but the oral tradition preserved an unbroken vein of tradition that carried on the message of the existence of that ancient society. And this message is still taken up by new generations of scholars, artists, and politicians in their desire to reinforce and mould the Finnish or the Karelian identity.

Partial Repentance of a Critic

The *Kalevala,* Politics, and the United States

BY WILLIAM A. WILSON

Whenever I write or talk about the *Kalevala,* I remember the words of the poet Eino Leino, written in preparation for the annual "*Kalevala* Day" celebration in 1917:

To honor the Kalevala *is to us Finns the same as honoring one's own deepest being; to come to know the* Kalevala *is the same as rejoicing over the swelling, streaming sunshine of one's own breast, over faith in life and over fulfillment. If a Finn does not care to read the* Kalevala, *then that testifies that he does not care to glance at the pages of his own book of destiny; if a Finn does not like the* Kalevala, *then that testifies that he does not like anything nor anybody, for only one who loves his own primeval self can radiate love around him. But if a Finn ridicules the* Kalevala, *then that is a sin against the Holy Ghost.*[1]

If the burden of paying proper homage to the *Kalevala* is heavy for the Finn, it is

doubly so for the foreigner like myself who chooses to write about the *Kalevala* or about *Kalevala* scholarship. Almost from the day of its publication the *Kalevala* became for the Finns a major witness to the country's noble past and the primary evidence that Finland, long considered a backward and untalented nation, merited a place among the civilized nations of the world. Considering the immediate and enduring symbolic significance achieved by the *Kalevala* and the great national pride in the work, the Finns have taken with something less than good cheer any aspersions cast on the *Kalevala* or its compiler by outside writers.

For example, in 1902, on the occasion of Elias Lönnrot's hundredth birthday, the Swedish scholar K. B. Wiklund published articles on the *Kalevala* in both Sweden and Germany, pointing out what Finnish folklorists had known for several decades but what the general Finnish population would not fully grasp for some years to come—namely, that Finland's national epic was the literary creation not of the Finnish folk but of Elias Lönnrot and that it had been composed not in some distant antiquity but in the 1800s at Lönnrot's work table.[2] The Finnish popular press responded to this attack on the integrity of the *Kalevala* angrily. An editorial writer in *Uusi Suometar*, a leading nationalist newspaper, declared:

That scientist [Wiklund] who serves Uppsala University, [and] who in his two publications has particularly wanted to oppress the Finns, knows well how to serve other than scientific ends. And now the sourness he has sown is spreading in Germany—it has already pretty well poisoned Scandinavia; it will move from Germany to France, to England, and so on; and in a few years no foreigner will any longer believe that the Finnish nation has its own national epic.

But that must not happen! Dr. Wiklund's doctrine offends the national self consciousness of every Finn. It damages those good opinions which the educated in foreign lands hold about our people. Therefore, our scientific and professional men must pick up the pen and prove this "Wiklundism" to be without doubt a fabricated scientific lie.[3]

Wiklund's sin, in my opinion, was not so much that he had questioned the authenticity of the *Kalevala*, but that he had done so as a foreigner. Finns might quarrel among themselves about the nature of the *Kalevala*, but foreigners were supposed to admire and praise the work.

I have had some experience in this area myself. When I published *Folklore and Nationalism in Modern Finland*,[4] I was soon taken to task for saying what I had heard Finnish scholars say with impunity. For example, in 1914 Kaarle Krohn abandoned his mythological interpretation of Finnish epic poetry and began to view the heroes of the poetry as historical figures who had once walked as free men on free Finnish soil and had with the sword won fame and honor for the fatherland.[5] When Jouko Hautala, in his history of Finnish folklore scholarship, pointed out that Krohn's changed view was motivated in part by the politically charged spirit of the time,[6] no

one, to my knowledge, seemed unduly troubled. But when I said essentially the same thing, when I argued that the image of the past reflected in the mirror of Finnish folk poetry has very often been shaped by the political predisposition of the scholar holding the mirror, I raised the hair on the backs of several Finnish necks.

Writing about the *Kalevala* as a foreigner, I certainly have no desire to sin against the Holy Ghost, to deprive the Finns of any honor which is justly theirs, or to stir anyone to anger. I would like instead, first, to pay brief tribute to what I consider the uncontestable contributions of Elias Lönnrot and his epic and, second, to reassess criticisms I have made earlier of the Finns and, where possible, to apply these criticisms now to the United States. As Elli Köngäs Maranda has noted, speaking of my work, "It is easier to criticize one's colleagues in a far-away country than it is to criticize colleagues closer to home, or oneself."[7] In what follows I will focus on colleagues closer to home, and on myself. Hence the title of this essay. What I am repenting of, and why that repentance is only partial, will, I hope, become clear as I proceed.

But first, my tribute to the *Kalevala:* Perhaps the greatest contribution of the epic has been its impact on Finnish cultural awareness and national identity and on the country's movement toward independence. At the beginning of the nineteenth century, Finland faced an uncertain future. Lacking the binding ties of a common language, a national literature, and a recognized history, the Finns were ill-prepared to face the century of attempted Russification of their country that lay ahead. Then in the 1820s, under the influence of Romantic ideals developing in the land, Elias Lönnrot began the folk poetry collecting expeditions that would eventually help reverse these circumstances and give the Finns sorely needed faith in themselves and hope for their future.

On the basis of information contained in the poems he had collected, Lönnrot began gradually to develop in his mind a picture of a noble Finnish antiquity, a vision of two great nations—Kalevala and Pohjola—of renowned Finnish heroes—Väinämöinen, Ilmarinen, Lemminkäinen—and of their famous deeds. Using lines drawn from the poems, almost as one uses words drawn from his own language, Lönnrot stitched together a poetic narrative which brought his own romantic vision of the past to the awareness of his countrymen and gave them in the process a priceless possession, a national epic.[8]

What Lönnrot did was create poems similar to what he imagined the poets of ancient Finland had once sung. He never claimed that he had reconstructed the original poems nor that from fragmented parts he had restored to the people a once unified epic whole. But his enthusiastic countrymen, seeking grist for their romantic-nationalistic mills, believed he had—a belief that persisted among scholars for several decades and among the general populace well into this century. The *Kalevala* thus became the charter for the burgeoning nationalistic movement, providing impetus, as Lauri Honko has noted, for a wide variety of activities:

It cannot be denied that particularly in the spheres of political history . . . [the Kalevala's] impact has been great—to say nothing of the fact that it was strongly influential in virtually all areas of science, that it gave birth to new branches of science, that it enriched the Finnish language and laid the foundation stone for Finnish literature, and, finally, that for the first time it drew the name of Finland on the world map. An epic and only an epic could achieve this—[it could not have been achieved] by even the best of some other form of folklore publication.[9]

No one can know, of course, what might have happened had Lönnrot not published the *Kalevala*. What does seem clear is that the epic and the cultural and artistic works based on it contributed significantly to the national self-awareness that made it possible for Finland to take advantage of unsettled world conditions in 1917 and to become an independent nation. At that time the Finns might have well recalled the words of Julius Krohn, pronounced three decades earlier:

Let us imagine a poor, unknown boy raised in the wilderness, who steps out into the world with a burning desire to take part in mankind's great battle for the promotion of everything beautiful, good, and noble. But all look at him with amazement, laugh at his unfamiliar movement, ask with scorn who he is that he imagines himself able to stand beside so many high-born and experienced heroes and [ask] how he can prove his ability [to perform] such great tasks. And then a good spirit suddenly puts in his hand a beautiful, brightly sparkling sword, a legacy of his father, at the same time an unquestionable witness of his royal lineage and a powerful weapon for his own future heroic deeds. And . . . [then] the scorn and laughter change to respect [and] fascination, and the young man himself feels his shyness giving way to hopeful bravery. Let us picture all this; only then can we fully know what kind of gift Lönnrot has given his people in the Kalevala.[10]

The second major contribution of the *Kalevala* has been its influence on the development of folklore scholarship. Immediately following the publication of the epic, collecting efforts waned somewhat. But when questions of the authenticity of Lönnrot's work began to surface, collectors took to the field again, this time in search of the evidence that would exonerate Lönnrot. And thus began the collecting efforts that have continued to the present. The results have been, first, the establishment of one of the world's largest, and certainly one of the best, folklore archives; second, the publication from 1908 to 1948 of *Suomen kansan vanhat runot* (*The Ancient Poems of the Finnish People*), a thirty-three-volume collection of genuine folk poetry that speaks more eloquently of the Finnish people's spiritual and intellectual heritage than the *Kalevala* ever could; and, third, the development of an internationally recognized method of folklore research.

As early as the late 1700s, Lönnrot's precursor Henrik Gabriel Porthan had noted "that by comparing the differing variants [of poems] with each other, one can restore them to a more perfect and more suitable form."[11] As the collecting efforts in the second half of the nineteenth century brought in an increasing number of variants, scholars like A. A. Borenius and Julius and Kaarle Krohn put Porthan's suggestion to the test as they attempted to discover the age, origin, and distribution paths of the poems. In the process they developed the historical-geographical, or Finnish, method which for decades dominated scholarship in Finland and in the folklore world in general.[12] Today the method has fallen from favor, as researchers have sought answers to different kinds of questions. Still, we cannot gainsay the contribution of the method to the development of our discipline; it was the Finnish method that gave scientific respectability to subsequent folklore study.

A third contribution of Lönnrot and his followers was a self-sacrificing devotion to duty that could serve as a model for us all. I think, for example, of the young Daniel Europaeus, the great collector of Karelian and Ingrian poetry. When a friend wrote urging Europaeus to put aside his collecting and return to the university, he replied: "It would be wrong to put off to some indefinite time the work [of collecting], particularly now when there is a desire in my blood that will grant no rest until its demands have been met."[13] Most of all, I think of Lönnrot himself. During his lifetime, Lönnrot made eleven collecting expeditions, traveled some thirteen thousand miles, much of the time on foot and in backwoods areas, and collected sixty-five thousand lines of poetry. In 1835, with the first edition of the *Kalevala* finally completed, he wrote to the chairman of the Finnish Literature Society these simple and revealing words: "A lot of work these poems have been, but I'm not sorry, if they are at last suitable."[14]

When I first began to study the interrelationship of folklore studies and national aspirations in Finland, I intended to focus primarily on the nineteenth century, on the very praiseworthy contributions folklore study had made toward Finnish cultural—and even political—independence. Almost as an afterthought, I decided to look briefly at the twentieth century, particularly at the troubled period following Finnish independence between the two world wars. I did not like what I saw. In my judgment, during those years both Finnish nationalism and the folklore study that supported it in some instances shifted toward extremism. Briefly, the criticisms of this era I eventually published were threefold: first, that Finnish scholars knew perfectly well that the *Kalevala* was an epic created by Lönnrot but in their patriotic utterances to the general public often kept alive the romantic view that the *Kalevala* was a folk epic sprung from the heart and soul of the Finnish people and therefore revealing best what it really meant to be a Finn; second, that these same scholars tended at times to be patriots first and scholars second and therefore reached politically expedient research conclusions; and third, that some scholars and a host of propagandists used the *Kalevala* and the images of the past they found reflected there to rally people to the political causes they espoused. Lying behind these criticisms was my unstated assumption that the world is best served when the scholar remains in his study and does not soil his hands with what Europeans today might call *folklorismus* and what Americans would call applied folklore or public-sector folklore. *Folklorismus*, or "folklorism," briefly stated, is the process through which authentic folklore is drawn from the social settings in which it naturally occurs and then is presented, or performed, in a variety of different settings to satisfy political, economic, religious, entertainment, educational, or artistic ends.

Today, ten years after publishing my book and, I hope, ten years wiser, I still do not like what happened in Finland in the 1920s and 1930s. But I have come to hold a less judgmental view, and I have learned that what I observed in Finland is in many ways not so different from what exists in my own country.

It did not take me long after publishing the book to realize that probably no one writes free from political ideology, myself included. The distaste I had felt for the excessive Finnish nationalism of the interwar period was surely heightened by what I believed to be an excessive American nationalism that had led to American imperialism in Southeast Asia. And this belief probably influenced my writing. I did most of my research during the late 1960s, when American activity in Vietnam was escalating. Each morning, as I came to my desk in the ethnological library of the Finnish Literature Society, my good friend Matti Sarmela would greet me with the question, "No, mitenkä Vietnamissa menee?" (Well, how are things going in Vietnam?) Never able to come up with a defense for what seemed to me an indefensible policy, I would turn to the books laid out on my desk and read in them statements that seemed equally indefensible—patriotic, rhetorical statements in which Finnish scholar-patriots, using the *Kalevala* as their historical justification, argued for a militaristic posture and an expansionist foreign policy. I find those statements no more palatable today than I did then, but I have come to see them in a little less sinister light and realize that in many instances they were made by men and women motivated by a genuine and heartfelt concern for their ethnic kinsmen on the Soviet side of the border.

One reason why it was relatively easy for me to scorn applied folklore when I did my research was that in the United States work in applied and public folklore was only beginning and was generally seen in negative terms. In 1971, for example, in the American Folklore Society's annual meeting in Washington, a proposal was put forth to set up an applied folklore section of the society. The proposal was defeated. From that time to the present, in what Richard Dorson called a "folklore boom,"[15] there has been a remarkable turnaround. As early as 1967 the Smithsonian Institution began its annual Festival of American Folklife, and the same year the first state folklorist was hired in Pennsylvania to develop and coordinate public programs. But the big push came in the 1970s. In 1974 the Folk Arts Program was added to the National Endowment for the Arts, and federal money was thus made available throughout the country for a wide range of public folklore activities; in 1976 the American Folklife Center was created with the passage in Congress of the American Folklife Preservation Act; and in 1977 the Office of Folklife Programs was established at the Smith-

sonian Institution. Perhaps most important, the number of state folk arts coordinators has continued to increase. Some forty states now have coordinators, all of whom are engaged in public folklore work.

Equally remarkable, for me at least, has been my own involvement in public folklore activities. In 1971 I voted against the applied folklore proposal. In an article published in 1975, I wrote:

Should the folklorist be content simply to study the folk and their lore, or should he use his research to bring about social, political, economic, or religious change? Should he use the lore he collects and studies only to increase our understanding of and sympathy for the human condition, or should he attempt to use that lore to improve the lives of the people? . . . My own view is that the folklorist's best course lies in always being a scholar first and a patriot or special pleader second—not because the cause one pleads is not worthy, but because his duty to it too easily clouds his vision and allows him to see only that which serves his ideological ends.[16]

I had scarcely sent these words to the printer when some ironical god decided to change my life. Early in 1976, the same year my book on folklore and nationalism in Finland was published, I received a call from Suzi Jones asking me to locate Utah folk artists and crafts people to perform in the Bicentennial Festival of American Folklife in Washington. My life has never again been the same. Since 1976 I have received two grants from the National Endowment for the Arts to find local folk artists and present them in folk festivals; I have worked on several projects for the American Folklife Center; I have served three years on the Folk Arts Panel of the National Endowment for the Arts, and a fourth year as its chairman; I serve currently as chairman of the Utah Folklife Center and on the board of directors of the Utah Arts Council; I am on the American Folklore Society's Centennial Coordinating Committee, whose task is to plan a year-long celebration of the society and of American folklore; and I have done more consulting on public folklore projects than I care to remember.

Through this work, I have come to be-

Burlon Craig demonstrates his skill as a potter at the Smithsonian's Festival of American Folklife on the Mall in Washington, D.C. Mr. Craig was awarded a National Heritage Fellowship by the Folk Arts Program of the National Endowment for the Arts in 1984. Photograph by Dane Penland. Copyright © Smithsonian Institution 1981

lieve that the statement I made in 1975 is wrong. What one should be first and foremost is not necessarily a scholar, a patriot, or a special pleader—but a human being who responds humanely and sympathetically to the needs of other human beings: the need to take pride in one's heritage, the need to find value in and recognition for creative and artistic achievement, the need to keep alive and to pass on to others the traditions that will enrich their lives. I have also learned that there are a lot of charlatans in our field, people who will traffic with these needs for their own pleasure and profit. I have come to believe, therefore, that since applied folklore, like it or not, is going to remain part of the American folklore scene, professional folklorists have an obligation to enter the arena, to make sure that work done is the very best possible and that the picture presented the public is as accurate as it can be.

This is not to say that I have not on occasion had to sacrifice my purist principles or make compromises that have come back to haunt my night hours. Indeed, after working all day on the Folk Arts Panel and awarding a variety of public folklore grants,

I have sometimes come back to my hotel and lain awake wondering if we should have awarded any grants at all. And it has certainly seemed to me that there are some issues those of us in public folklore should struggle with more directly. We get so involved in the work that we forget to stand aside now and then and ask some questions about what we are doing. On the basis of my earlier study of folklore pursuits in Finland and my ten years' work in public folklore, here are some questions I would ask:

Question 1: *Who speaks for folklore?* This is the question Richard Dorson asked during the debates over applied folklore. It is still a good question today. In Finland during the 1920s and 1930s, as I have pointed out, the political right, using the *Kalevala* as part of their argument, advocated building a strong military machine and expanding Finland's borders to include the song lands across the Soviet border from which Lönnrot and others had collected the old poems. The political left, using the same *Kalevala,* argued for the creation of a workers' paradise, a classless, communistic society. And each side made vitriolic attack on the other.

In this country the issues have perhaps been less dramatic but nevertheless just as real. In 1978, when the Department of the Interior and the Army Corps of Engineers asked the American Folklife Center to conduct a folklore project that would mitigate the cultural damage resulting from the Tennessee-Tombigbee Waterway Project, American folklorists lined up on each side of the issue. Former allies spoke hot words against each other, and former supporters of the center threatened to withdraw their support. In 1984, when the American Folklore Society, in its informational booklet, published a statement on organizational folklore,[17] some members of the society, claiming that research in organizational folklore would provide management with information that could be used against labor, charged the society with unethical behavior. It is fine to argue for applied folklore, but what happens when that lore is applied to ends some of us don't like? Who speaks for folklore?

Question 2: *How do we pull folklore from its context, as we do in almost every public presentation of folklore, and still give the public a fair notion of what folklore is?* In a recent publication, Matti Kuusi, speaking against those who "still look to Lönnrot's epic as a source of information about ancient Finnish poetry," said, "the results are as reliable as if Liszt were used as a primary source for research into Hungarian folk music."[18] I often wonder if American folklore, separated from the context which gives it life and meaning, and presented on the concert stage, at a folk festival, or in a museum display, gives a picture of American tradition any more accurate than Lönnrot's *Kalevala* gives of Finnish folk poetry. We use these presentations to awaken public interest in folklore, to strengthen identity, or to build pride in heritage; but, as most folklorists will know, we awaken public interest and build pride in something that does not in fact exist, except on the performance stage or at the festival. This does not strike me as too different from Finnish scholars—also to strengthen identity and build pride in heritage—helping keep alive among the general populace an image of the *Kalevala* as a mirror of the ancient Finnish spirit which the scholars themselves knew was not accurate.

Question 3: *Are we sufficiently aware of the ideological or value systems that shape our public folklore work?* Most people perceive the past in terms meaningful to them in the present. Thus Lönnrot saw in the old Finnish poems a glorious Finnish past that would give his countrymen, struggling toward national awareness, a model for future national development. Other Finns with other dreams have found in the *Kalevala* historical justification for other hopes and aspirations.

Don't we do the same thing? Archaeologist Mark Leone, speaking of living history exhibits, states:

As visitor you take all this folklore and this symbol mongering and imagine yourself to be the native of Williamsburg or Mesa Verde. . . . And because the data are relatively mute . . . , they are then more easily made to give the message of those doing

*the reconstructing. . . . The tourist [at Wil-
liamsburg] does not really become immersed in the eighteenth century at all; he
is spared the shock of the filth, degradation,
and misery common to that era, and is led
into a fake eighteenth century, a creation
of the twentieth. While in this altered frame
of mind he is faced with messages—the re-
inforcement of modern American values like
those surrounding the myths of our own
origin as a nation—that come out of today,
not two centuries ago.*[19]

Archaeology in the service of national goals
is not particularly offensive, says Leone, but
what is offensive "is the archeologists' un-
awareness of this function."[20] Leone was
speaking of living history presentations, but
what he says applies equally well to public
presentations of contemporary folklore.
Again, I ask the question: How aware are
we public folklorists (and I include myself
in the group) of the ideological values that
inform our work? When I did field work
for the American Folklife Center in Paradise Valley, Nevada, I soon discovered a
number of cracks in paradise. I was told by
my supervisor that if I included negative
statements in my report, he would edit them
out. We cannot, he said, give negative
impressions in a study funded by the public
and made available to the public, including
the people of Paradise Valley. In our public
presentations of folklore it is common
practice, I believe, to focus on the positive,
on the smiling aspects, of traditional culture and to "edit out" the rest. When we
do so, what are the messages we are giving?
It is time, I think, to stand aside and take
a calm, detached look at the ends we are
serving. Good intentions do not always bring
good results—in Finland or in the United
States.

Question 4: *In our presentations of folklore, have we put too much emphasis on
the particular groups that keep the lore alive?*
In the introduction to a book on Finnish
proverbs, Matti Kuusi once wrote: "What
kind of people actually are we? What is the
Finnish national character?" He continued:
"There really is something that separates us
from Italians, Americans, Russians, even
from the Swedes."[21] He then explained that

he would use Finnish proverbs to identify
the Finnish national character and to cast
it in sharp relief.

In America our focus is not so much on
the national character but rather on the
character of the different groups that make
up our pluralistic society; however, the attempt to discover the uniqueness of the
group is closely parallel to the attempt to
discover the uniqueness of the Finnish nation. Thus the brochure for the Folk Arts
Program of the National Endowment for
the Arts states: "The folk and traditional
arts have grown through time within the
many groups that make up any nation—
groups that share the same ethnic heritage,
language, occupation, religion or geographic area. The homegrown traditional
artistic activities of such groups are sometimes called folk arts, and they serve both
to identify and to symbolize the group that
originated them."[22]

There is nothing wrong with either Kuusi's
statement or the statement in the Folk Arts
Panel brochure. They fall squarely in the
center of mainline folklore study. But it
seems to me there are better approaches to
take. Instead of focusing on what makes us
different from each other, why not stress
that which unites us. In *Folklife Center
News,* Alan Jabbour said that "our professional field has tilted too far in recent years
toward emphasizing the ethnographic
present and stressing the group-factor over
the time-factor in tradition."[23] I agree. The
great value of the *Kalevala* is that it illu-
minates not just the Finnish spirit but also
the human spirit. Like all good literature it
confronts again and again those enduring
human problems with which human beings
have always struggled. For me, the great
value of folklore is that it does the same
thing—that's why folklore is essentially a
humanistic discipline. When we focus our
attention primarily on what it means to be
a Finn or on what it means to be a member
of a particular American ethnic, occupational, religious, or regional group, we limit
our vision and miss that which is most important in what we study.

I am convinced that we generate and
transmit folklore not because we belong to
a particular nation or to a particular group

Tlingit dancers from the village of Angoon, Alaska, perform during "Celebration 84," a biennial event sponsored by the Sealaska Heritage Foundation. The Traditional Native Arts Program at the Alaska State Council on the Arts prompted the first celebration in 1982 by providing seed money for the production of a regional event that would promote traditional Native dance in southeast Alaska. Since 1980 the program has directly supported and encouraged the development and preservation of Alaska's traditional Native arts. Photograph by Suzi Jones, Alaska State Council on the Arts

but because we are human beings coming to terms with recurring human problems in traditional human ways. To be sure, this folklore is expressed in and is given color by the groups to which we belong; it can serve, therefore, as a means of understanding and increasing our sympathy for these groups. But the source of the lore, we should always remember, lies not in the groups, not in our differences, but in our common humanity, in our common human struggle to endure.

My repentance, then, is partial but not complete. I still greatly admire both the *Kalevala* and its creator, Elias Lönnrot. I still admire the work of Finns who created almost an entire artistic culture on the basis of the *Kalevala*. I still look askance at the political uses made of the *Kalevala* in the 1920s and 1930s. But I have come to view these years more sympathetically, particu-

larly as I have struggled with some of the same problems in my own work. Perhaps if Elias Lönnrot were to return for a moment and look at the problems still facing us, he would give no advice to help us find our way but, with considerable sympathy, would simply recite again the words with which he closed his epic:

Siitäpä nyt tie menevi,
Ura uusi urkenevi
Laajemmille laulajoille,
Runsahammille runoille
Nuorisossa nousevassa,
Kansassa kasuavassa.

From here now the road goes on,
A new path opens up
For more capable singers,
For more abundant songs
Among the rising youth,
Among the growing generation.

NOTES

1. Eino Leino, "Kansallisviikko: Kalevala johtotähtenä," *Sunnuntai*, February 25, 1917, pp. 1–2.
2. See K. B. Wiklund, *Om Kalevala: Finnarnes nationalepos, och forskningarna rörande detsamma*, Föreningen Heimdals Folkskrifter, no. 71 (Stockholm, 1901).
3. "Kalevala-tutkimuksen tulokset," *Uusi Suometar*, November 6, 1901, p. 2.
4. William A. Wilson, *Folklore and Nationalism in Modern Finland* (Bloomington: Indiana University Press, 1976).
5. Kaarle Krohn, "Kaleva und seine Sippe," *Suomalais-Ugrilaisen Seuran Aikakauskirja* 30, no. 35 (1914). Krohn developed these ideas in full four years later in *Kalevalankysymyksiä: Opas kansan vanhojen runojen tilaajille ja käyttäjille ynnä suomalaisen kansanrunojen opiskelijoille ja harrastajille*, 2 vols., special issues of *Suomalais-Ugrilaisen Seuran Aikakauskirja* 35–36 (1918).
6. See Jouko Hautala, *Finnish Folklore Research 1828–1919* (Helsinki, 1969), 117, 134, 140.
7. Elli Kögäs Maranda, "Review of *Folklore and Nationalism in Modern Finland*," *Western Folklore* 37 (1978): 66.
8. The best treatment of Lönnrot's composition of the *Kalevala* is Väinö Kaukonen, *Lönnrot ja Kalevala* (Helsinki, 1979).
9. Lauri Honko, "Suomalainen kansalliseepos," *Seulottua sanaa: Kirjoituksia sanataiteen, kielen, ja kansanperinteen alalta*, Suomalaisen Kirjallisuuden Seuran Toimituksia, no. 269 (Helsinki, 1960), 209.
10. Cited in Martti Haavio, "Kalevalakultti," in *Kalevala kansallinen aarre: Kirjoitelmia kansalliseepoksen vaiheilta*, ed. F. A. Hästesko and Martti Haavio (Porvoo, 1949), 248.
11. Henrik Gabriel Porthan, *Suomalaisesta runoudesta*, in *Henrik Gabriel Porthanin tutkimuksia*, vol. 1 of *Suomalaisuuden syntysanoja*, Suomalaisen Kirjallisuuden Seuran Toimituksia, no. 105 (Helsinki, 1904), 99–100.
12. For a discussion of the Finnish school, see Hautala, 62–171.
13. A. R. Niemi, ed., *D.E.D. Europaeuksen kirjeitä ja matkakertomuksia*, Suomi, 4th ser., vol. 3, no. 1 (Helsinki, 1905), 97.
14. Letter to C. N. Keckman, February 6, 1835, cited in Kaukonen, 59.
15. Richard M. Dorson, "The Folklore Boom," *Journal of the Folklore Institute* 12 (1975): 152.
16. William A. Wilson, "The *Kalevala* and Finnish Politics," *Journal of the Folklore Institute* 12 (1975): 152.
17. American Folklore Society, "Folklore and Organizational Life," *Folklore/Folklife* (Washington, 1984), 14.
18. Matti Kuusi, "Introduction," *Finnish Folk Poetry, Epic: An Anthology in Finnish and English*, ed. Matti Kuusi, Keith Bosley, Michael Branch (Helsinki, 1977), 32.
19. Mark P. Leone, "Archeology as the Science of Technology: Mormon Town Plans and Fences," in *Research and Theory in Current Archeology*, ed. Charles L. Redman (New York: John Wiley & Sons, 1973), 130–131.
20. Ibid., 133.
21. Matti Kuusi, *Vanhan kansan sananlaskuviisaus* (Helsinki, 1953), v.
22. National Endowment for the Arts, *Folk Arts 85/86* (Washington, 1985), 1.
23. Alan Jabbour, "Director's Column," *Folklife Center News* 7, no. 4 (October–December 1984): 3.

Immigrant to Ethnic

Symbols of Identity Among Finnish-Americans

BY YVONNE HIIPAKKA LOCKWOOD

The United States is a country of many ethnic groups, each of which has maintained its separate identity. These communities, however, are not identical to ones in their countries of origin and, like all culture, are in a constant state of change. Subsequent to the resettlement period in this country, and in fact even during immigration, new settlers were influenced in many ways that resulted in a change from immigrant to ethnic status. The Finns, for example, were no longer Finns nor were they Americans, but rather they were Finnish-Americans.

Ethnicity and ethnic identity are topics that have occupied the attention of scholars for almost two decades, and folklorists have examined how traditions of ethnic groups are a gauge of acculturation and culture maintenance and how folklore is used to differentiate one group from another. Spe-

Sauna of log construction in the Upper Peninsula. Photograph courtesy of the Folk Arts Division, Michigan State University Museum

A sauna in Michigan's Up-per Peninsula. Especially in rural areas, the sauna tends to be a separate building located behind or to the side of a house, and the siding on the sauna often matches the siding on the house. Photograph by Yvonne Lockwood

cific traditional culture traits often represent different stages of acculturation and degrees of cultural maintenance. Sauna, pasty, and St. Urho are markers of Finnish-American ethnic boundaries, and individuals identify themselves and are identified by others as Finnish-American according to their participation in these cultural forms of expression. The *Kalevala*, on the other hand, is a part of Finnish national culture; but during the sesquicentennial year of the publication of this epic, questions have been raised about its role in Finnish-American culture.

There has never been a question about sauna, the Finnish hot air bath—often called steam bath in colloquial English (the term refers both to the place where one bathes and to the act of bathing): sauna is one of the most common and essential expressions of Finnish-American culture.

Because of the sauna's traditional associations with the life cycle, it is not surprising that during the period of immigration and resettlement, the first building constructed was often a sauna. It was here that mothers gave birth, boys and girls bathed in preparation for marriage, and elders were prepared for burial. The sauna provided a sense of order and stability in the disrupted lives of immigrants, but Finns in the United States quickly became aware of how others perceived sauna behavior. Because Finns rolled in the snow, jumped into icy lakes and rivers, or at the very least stood naked outside the sauna to cool down, non-Finns were suspicious and reported to local authorities that the newcomers worshipped pagan gods and performed dances while naked outside their strange log houses. This association, although no longer regarded as religiously motivated, still contributes to a certain stereotype of tough and gutsy Finns, as well as to an awareness by Finnish-Americans of their own uniqueness.

Hilda Hellen in front of her sauna, Gogebic County, Michigan, 1981. Photograph by Yvonne Lockwood

Above: Lauri Lipponen at the door of a sauna dressing room with a home-made sauna dipper. Photograph courtesy of the Folk Arts Division, Michigan State University Museum

Above right: The interior of a sauna in the Upper Peninsula. Photograph courtesy of the Folk Arts Division, Michigan State University Museum

Below right: Interior of sauna in Kaleva, Michigan, 1985. Photograph by Yvonne Lockwood

Associations with life cycle events and rites of passage are seldom linked to sauna today. However, Finnish-Americans believe that sauna bathing transforms situations of disorder to order—for example, it can change illness to health, drunkenness to sobriety, anger to calm, and weakness to strength. In cases of illness and drunkenness, for example, sauna is the recommended folk remedy. The degree to which such a transformation is merely psychological and temporary is not relevant. Rather, the point is that the belief in the magic of the sauna is widespread, and to participate in sauna is the Finnish way to restore order.

Sauna also provides the context for learning about other aspects of the Finnish worldview. As in many cultures, adults are the agents of social order. In the sauna, adults teach young children values and attitudes about health, cleanliness, morals, and behavior. Thus sauna, as a place and as an enactment, is important in the enculturation of Finnish-American children.

There has been a proliferation of saunas in the western world since the 1950s, and they can be found in most urban centers of the United States. In Detroit, for example, one sees Bangkok Sauna, Pancho's Siesta Sauna, and Japanese Sauna, and there are also those found in motels, hotels, and physical fitness centers. From the perspective of Finnish-Americans, however, these are not real saunas: the users talk too loudly, wear bathing suits, and in general behave improperly. Moreover, these places are not hot enough.

The adoption of saunas by the mainstream American culture has strengthened a conscious association with sauna among Finnish-Americans, whereby the social function of the Finnish-American sauna has become the manifestation and reassertion of Finnish-American ethnic identity. But it is important to distinguish between the role of sauna in areas of dense Finnish-American population, such as the Lake Superior region of Michigan, Wisconsin, and Minnesota (where approximately 80 percent of the Finns have saunas), and in areas where Finnish-Americans are not numerous and are, perhaps, more assimilated into mainstream American culture. The role of sauna in densely populated Finnish-American communities has not waned. Despite showers and bathtubs, individuals sauna often and regularly. And one sees along lakeshores a growing number of *savu* saunas, romanticized smoke bath houses of the immigrant generation. In areas where there are fewer Finnish-Americans, sauna is experiencing a revival and is also being accepted by other Americans. But there it is usually not an integrated part of the regular pattern of life—rather it is a special entertainment and an act of self-conscious Finnishness.

Whereas sauna is a Finnish cultural transplant, the eating of pasty is a cultural trait adopted from another ethnic group, the Cornish. The pasty is a turnover of pie-like crust filled with a variety of food combinations. Wherever else the Cornish settled, the pasty is regarded as a Cornish specialty. What is called a Cornish pasty elsewhere is an Upper Peninsula pasty in Michigan, for pasty's symbolic meaning changed from ethnic to multiethnic and finally to regional. But pasty is often regarded as Finnish, and the explanation can be found in the history of the region.

After Michigan gained statehood in 1837, the state's Upper Peninsula experienced the first major mining boom in the United States—even before the gold rush—and early Cornish immigrants played a major role. Arriving in the United States with deep-mining techniques and experience, they set the pattern of mine work in the Upper Peninsula. By the time of mass migration at the end of the nineteenth and the beginning of the twentieth centuries, the Cornish were well-established in the mines as skilled workers, foremen, and mining captains. The later immigrants (Finns, Italians, Poles, Croats, and Serbs) provided the unskilled labor. The Cornish also established the patterns of social and cultural life, and new immigrants looked upon the Cornish as established Americans. They had status and their lives became models for what was regarded as American life.

Cultural geographers and anthropologists have argued that in the United States the first European or American white population to establish itself in an area usually defines the cultural patterns of the region. In Michigan the earlier immigrants of northern Europe sometimes established the cultural patterns adopted by the later-arriving immigrants from southern and eastern Europe. It was their neighborhoods into which new immigrants settled, and they who were most likely to be the foremen and supervisors in the mills and mines where the immigrants went to work. In the Upper Peninsula the influence of earlier immigrants on the emerging ethnic culture is most apparent in the pasty.

The pasty is the national dish of Cornwall, and it continues to play an important role in the diet of Cornish-Americans wherever they settled. It was quickly adopted by newer immigrants who worked with the Cornish in the mines of the Upper Peninsula. Not just a recipe but an entire cultural complex passed from individual to individual and from one ethnic group to another:

Right: Finlandia Bakery and Restaurant in Marquette, Michigan, where pasty is a specialty. Photograph courtesy of the Folk Arts Division, Michigan State University Museum

Opposite page, above: Making pasties. Photograph by Yvonne Lockwood.

Opposite page, below: Maxine Tarvin, a former Upper Peninsula resident who now lives in Ohio, in her kitchen with a tray of pasties. Photograph by Yvonne Lockwood

the uses, the way of eating, the practice of marking individual pasties, and so on.

The particular use of the Cornish pasty was an important reason for its being so readily adopted by members of the other ethnic groups in the Upper Peninsula. Both in Cornwall and among Cornish-Americans, the pasty was traditionally associated with work and, in particular, with mining. A pasty is easily carried in a pail or specially made sack, it retains its heat for a long time, it is eaten with the hands, and it makes a hearty meal by itself. Little wonder that the Finns, Italians, and Slavs who saw their Cornish foreman eating pasty soon were demanding it for themselves.

The Cornish, however, are a relatively small component of the Upper Peninsula. The first of the more predominant immigrants, the Finns, began to arrive in 1864, well after the main Cornish immigration but thirty years before the massive Finnish immigration. By 1880 foreign-born Finns numbered over one thousand. It probably was from these earlier Finnish immigrants, rather than from the Cornish themselves, that later Finnish arrivals adopted the pasty.

Some Finnish immigrants may have had their first experience with certain regional dishes of Finland in the American context. For example, *piiraat* and *kukko* resemble pasty. The existence in Finland of this similar food may have meant easier adoption of the pasty in the Michigan context. How, for example, was a newly arrived Finn to know that the pasty in the lunchpail of a fellow countryman who arrived some thirty years before was not merely a regional variant of food in Finland that he was already familiar with? In this way many Finns came to believe that pasty was a Finnish food.

Because of education and mass media, the pasty is known in the Upper Peninsula to be of Cornish origin. But its popular association with Finns cannot be totally ignored. For example, Raymond Sokolov, a former Michigan resident and ethnoculinary journalist, writes of the "Finnish flavor" of the pasty. Among some Upper Peninsula Finns themselves, the pasty is regarded as Finnish food. This belief is perpetuated by family tradition, Finnish "ethnic" church suppers, and annual Finnish

traditional celebrations, where pasty is a featured Finnish specialty. In addition to the historical role of the Finns in the diffusion of the pasty and the existence of a similar food in Finland, the Finnish association is further reinforced by the predominance of Finns in the Upper Peninsula. Here, then, is an example of cultural influences melting and mixing to shape a culture trait. Pasty is transformed from a monoethnic (Cornish) food to a multiethnic food, and concurrently to a regional specialty.

Because of the sesquicentennial celebration of the *Kalevala*, increased attention to this epic has raised questions about its role in Finnish-American culture and identity. By the time of mass migration from Finland, the *Kalevala* had become the symbol of the Finnish character and soul. It was evidence of a heroic people and proud past that was studied by school children. Other than its presence in the schools, we do not know its effect on average Finns. Nor do

we know the role, if any, it played in the lives of Finnish immigrants. What we do know is that new arrivals faced intellectual racism and political oppression in their new homeland that was fueled by a growing nativism among the established citizens. Oppressed from without, the Finnish community was also polarized within by a rivalry between the white Finns (conservative, bourgeois, and church-oriented) and the red Finns (left-wing socialists and later communists). Finns found strength and comfort in organizations such as cooperatives, workmen's circles, temperance societies, benevolent societies, and the church—organizations that often were aligned with one faction or the other. It was in the context of these organizations, with their choirs, theater groups, and sports clubs, that Finns maintained and reinforced their identity as Finns and as Finnish-Americans. Their differing ideologies very likely influenced their attitude to the *Kalevala* as well. The more conservative had a tendency to look to the past for meaning and direction, whereas those with left leanings tended to look to the future and a new and ideal society.

One of the early conservative organizations in the Finnish community was the Lodge of the Knights and Ladies of the Kaleva. The lodge was modeled after the secret society of the Masons and was created in 1887 in Belt, Montana, by a small group of men who were concerned about the image Finns were projecting of themselves to their neighbors. Too many Finns, they believed, indulged in drinking, brawling, and political struggle and held in contempt the old cultural values that the organizers cherished as basic to Finnishness. The resulting Knights of the Kaleva saw themselves as brokers of Finnish culture. Like the scholar-patriots of Finland, they turned to the *Kalevala* as a reflection of the genius of Finnish character, that is, wisdom, endurance, and bravery. Clearly the lodge founders, if not a product of this teaching, were influenced by the symbolism of the *Kalevala*.

At its zenith, there were some sixty lodges in the United States. Today there are about twenty-four. The fact that the lodge was a secret organization worked against its goal of unifying the community and eventually led to its own decline. According to Finns, ministers of churches attempted to dissuade their congregations from joining the lodges, and workers joined temperance societies and workmen's circles instead. Churches and political organizations began to sponsor their own summer schools and camps where Finnish language, history, and culture were taught.

On the other hand, the lodge promoted the *Kalevala* among its members and the general public. Copies of the epic, for example, were given to initiates, and the lodge's fraternal magazine, the *Kalevainen,* included articles and information about the *Kalevala*. The *Kalevala* was also donated to public and school libraries. Lodges around the country have sponsored annual programs that include readings from the epic and skits performed on the basis of it to commemorate the *Kalevala* on the anniversary of its publication. These events are open to the public and even in the early decades were well attended by the Finnish community. However, there is no evidence that these annual celebrations had a significant effect on the general Finnish public.

While the epic has not been popular, there are singular examples of awareness of the *Kalevala*. In Michigan and Minnesota, for example, one finds towns named Kaleva and streets named after heroes and places in the epic. Kaleva, Michigan, was plotted in 1900 by one Jacob Saari, a land developer who advertised through a Finnish-language newspaper to attract Finns already in the United States and Canada and in Finland to settle this new town. He named the town and the streets after the *Kalevala*. Six two-by-eight-foot murals painted by the WPA for the public school depicted scenes from the *Kalevala*.

I once asked a sampling of individuals in Michigan about their awareness of the *Kalevala* so as to get an indication of the extent to which the *Kalevala* has or has not become part of their lives. They included Ph.D.'s and grade school and high school graduates, activists in cultural organizations and Finnish-American studies, individuals who no longer live in Finnish communities, first generation to third generation, Finnish-American poets, and average working-class family members. In general, the *Kalevala* was known to be the national epic of Finland, a fact some learned only as middle-aged adults. Only a few had read the epic and then only in the last ten years. In the case of a second-generation poet, the epic was brought to her attention by her non-Finnish college professor.

While the *Kalevala* has not been important to a great number of Finns in the United States, some individuals have been inspired by it and regard it as a source of culture. For example, pride in the *Kalevala* has been expressed by some in terms of its link to *Hiawatha*, regarded as the epic of North America, and significantly, that part of North America where the largest number of Finns settled. It is believed by some that Longfellow depended heavily on the *Kalevala* when composing his epic. Such a belief has significant implications for Finnish-American identity. If the *Kalevala* does, in fact, contain the truth and wisdom of Finnish culture, reliance on it to express the soul of another culture further validates the worth of Finnish culture and of the *Kalevala* as an example of venerable world literature.

Longfellow, however, was only partially influenced by the *Kalevala*. The meter of *Hiawatha* is after the German adaptation of the Finnish, and the texts are based not on the *Kalevala* but on Schoolcraft's collection of Native American legends and myths. Longfellow did select some of these legends over others because they were similar to the *Kalevala*, which made structuring his epic easier because he too arranged unlinked narrative in linear structure, a literary license that gave unity to otherwise discrete unrelated narratives. Ultimately, Longfellow's *Hiawatha* is an example of nineteenth-century Romanticism, and the *Kalevala* was just a convenient model.

With accelerated publicity about the sesquicentennial of the *Kalevala*, Finnish-Americans are becoming more aware of this epic and its importance in world literature. Finnish cultural centers are sponsoring study circles on the *Kalevala* that are facilitated by local college and university non-Finnish professors. In Finland people admire the epic greatly but read it very little; its role in Finnish-American life may well take the same course.

The legend of St. Urho offers another example of the weakness of the *Kalevala* influence in this country. When Finnish-Americans of Minnesota created this cultural hero, their model was not a hero from the *Kalevala* but rather St. Patrick. And St. Urho looks more like a Finnish-American Paul Bunyan than an ancient Karelian hero. As details of this hero developed, legends explained that he was buried on the grounds of the Finn Creek Open Air Museum in Minnesota. Unlike Väinämöinen and heroes of other cultures who retreat to secluded places from which they will reappear when needed, St. Urho was not expected to reappear. Recently, however, and possibly as the result of increased awareness about the *Kalevala*, a "rumor" emerged that St. Urho's bones were scattered in a river. Supposedly, with a bit of magic, he can be brought back to life.

The pseudo-legend of St. Urho was written in the 1950s by a Finnish-American psychology professor in Minnesota. St. Urho is said to have saved Finland's vineyards from a plague of grasshoppers or frogs. As a joke, a small group of Finnish-Americans transformed this legend into a community celebration of Finnish-Americanness. St. Urho is called the patron saint of Finnish-Americans; he is not known in Finnish tradition, yet his deed of bravery is set in Finland.

Over the years, activities commemorating St. Urho have expanded to fill an entire day and evening with parades, Finnish-American food, toboggan and ski races, "Finlander" joke telling, dancing to Finnish-American music, drinking green beer and grape juice, and dressing in outrageous green and purple costumes. In the Great Lakes region, one sees motels, beer, bumper stickers, T-shirts, and buttons in the name of St. Urho. In Minnesota a larger-than-life-size sculpture commemorates this folk hero. Fifty states have recognized March 16 as St. Urho's Day, and Finnish-Americans are now lobbying to make this day a national holiday.

The symbols for St. Urho's celebration are intentionally the same as the Irish St. Patrick's: the color green, the saint as hero, and his rescue of a country from devastation. Most important, however, is the fact that St. Urho's Day is the day before St. Patrick's Day. The manner in which festivities are enacted is also of interest. Much of the activity is in jest; people act silly and speak in exaggerated dialect stereotypic of the immigrant generation. The jokes, if told by anyone other than Finnish-Americans, would be ethnic slurs.

Although some Finnish-Americans are outraged by the celebration and refuse to participate, and even some Irish-Americans have voiced complaint, the popularity of St. Urho's Day continues to grow. St. Urho has become a symbol of Finnish-American culture whose celebration is intended to attract attention to Finnish-Americans and to differentiate their Finnishness from Anglo-Saxon influences. Despite its contrived origin, the celebration and the hero have become traditional through collective ceremony.

Festivals can be the context in which ethnicity is expressed symbolically. Festivals can also be an expression of the new ethnicity—the quest for a meaningful past. It is not an indulgence in nostalgia or a romanticizing of the past, but rather a struggle for identity and a resistance against the perceived homogenization with mainstream American culture. People consciously attempt to revitalize their cultures by reestablishing ethnic differentiation based on cultural traits they have borrowed, inherited, reshaped, and even newly created. The festival celebration of St. Urho is just such an example of the new ethnicity. It becomes an antidote for cultural assimilation or social alienation.

Celebrations and ceremonies are ways to deal with the past. Historically the Finnish-American community was divided between "church" and "red" Finns, divisions rooted in political and class ideology. St. Urho's celebration brings together both factions and mediates the difference between them. The celebration's license for outrageous behavior and laughter momentarily destroys the differences and allows for a new beginning. Just as the celebration has revitalized the Finnish-American community, it is also encouraging participation from other ethnics. In the Upper Peninsula, for example, an Irishman has maintained St. Urho tradition in one town for a decade by planning and hosting the celebration. In another town, local Irish participate in the festivities dressed in shamrock green and protest St. Urho's Day in good fun.

St. Urho's celebration, as collective ceremony, has certain power to propagate and shape ideas. Not only does the celebration ignite feelings of Finnishness, it also has the potential to revive resentments caused by past interethnic relations. However, Irish participation seems to deflect strong negativism. Laughter and funmaking exaggerate the collectivity and cooperation, and the juxtaposed symbols give a sense of unity.

St. Urho's celebration is a convergence of different traditions that reflect a stage in the ethnic process and inform us of regional history and culture. The event provides the context for the performance of a variety of Finnish-American traditions and sets the

Al Jokela, with a green beard, tells a "Finlander" joke at the annual St. Urho's Day celebration, Rock, Michigan, 1981. Photograph by Jenny Lancour

History cannot be ignored in the meaning of this event. We are reminded that in the mining and lumber industries of the north country, the English and Irish often had the better jobs, better homes, and positions of power, whereas Finns felt like second-class citizens. And the pressures to conform to the way of life established by the earlier immigrants were great. Thus, St. Urho is the Finnish-American response to the Irish. By exaggerating cultural traits designated as Finnish-American, participants momentarily express freedom from foreign influence and stress Finnish heritage.

Mike Aalto, Ruth Winkelbauer, and Gary Wellman judging the Finnish joke-telling contest, Rock, Michigan, 1981. Behind the judges is a poster of St. Urho chasing a grasshopper. Photograph by Jenny Lancour

Jerry Maki dressed as a frog, his wife, Sharon, dressed in purple and green colors as a cheerleader, Mary Westlund dressed as a bunch of purple grapes, and her husband, Craig, as green grapes, St. Urho's Day celebration, Rock, Michigan, 1981. Photograph by Jenny Lancour

stage for Finns to come together and publicly declare that they are "proud to be Finnish-Americans."

The legacy of the change from Finnish immigrant to Finnish-American ethnic status is presented in a selection of Finnish-American traditions: sauna, an immigrant transplant; pasty, an adopted and adapted food; and St. Urho, a fictitious folk hero. Sauna and St. Urho are unquestionably Finnish-American traditions and reflect different degrees of acculturation and Finnish cultural maintenance. The ethnic association of pasty, on the other hand, is secondary to that of region. Although deeply rooted in Cornish ethnic tradition, it has become symbolic of the entire Upper Peninsula, as well as being adopted by and attributed to Finnish-Americans. Despite this apparent ambiguity, regional and ethnic identities are seldom in conflict, because they exist at different levels. For example, the Finnish claim to pasty will rarely be made in a context when it could be argued that it is regional or Cornish.

The influence of the *Kalevala* on Finnish-American identity is in a process of change. The recent attention to the *Kalevala* has fostered claims that the epic has nurtured Finnish-American values, but the evidence proves quite the opposite—a very small proportion of the Finns in the United States are (and were) familiar with this epic. But the publicity has generated new interest. The rhetoric of some educated leaders of the community is not unlike that of nineteenth-century Finns who strove to create a sense of Finnish national identity. Disregarding the shamanistic implications of the epic, the Finns in the United States and Canada are discovering a heroic heritage that they claim as theirs. This wave of new ethnicity emphasizes another step in the ethnic process, that is, an attempt to develop stronger cultural ties with the country of origin, perhaps at a time when the link seems weak, by acknowledging the sharing of an ancient tradition.

FOR FURTHER READING

Before the work of Fredrik Barth, systematic anthropological studies of ethnicity were not numerous. Barth focused anthropological attention on this area of study, bringing together diverse ideas and establishing a foundation for subsequent research. See Fredrik Barth, *Ethnic Groups and Boundaries* (Boston: Little, Brown, 1969). For further reading on ethnicity, see Jonathan Okamura, "Situational Ethnicity," *Ethnic and Racial Studies* 4, no. 4 (1981): 452–65 and Herbert Gans, "Symbolic Ethnicity: The Future of Ethnic Groups and Cultures in America," *Ethnic and Racial Studies* 2, no. 1 (1979): 1–20. For an excellent overview of the subject, see Stephen Stern, "Ethnic Folklore and the Folklore of Ethnicity," *Western Folklore* 36, no. 1 (1977): 7–32.

I wish to acknowledge the contribution of William G. Lockwood to the development of the ideas on pasty in this paper. They are more fully developed in an article we coauthored, "The Cornish Pasty in Northern Michigan," in *Food in Motion: The Migration of Foodstuffs and Cookery Techniques,* ed. Alan Davidson (Leeds, England: Prospect Books, 1983), 83–94. See also my study "The Sauna: An Expression of Finnish-American Identity," *Western Folklore* 36, no. 1 (1977): 71–84.

Right: Al Jokela (right), organizer of the St. Urho's Day celebration in Rock, Michigan, partying with a friend, 1983. Photograph by Randy Lancour

Below: Al Soyring of Mc-Farland, Michigan, first place winner in the best costume contest, St. Urho's Day celebration, Rock, Michigan, 1983. Photograph by Jenny Lancour

Sledding pulpwood to the loading platform (LC-USF34-30670-D)

Minnesota Logging Camp, September 1937

A Photographic Series by Russell Lee

SELECTED AND INTRODUCED BY CARL FLEISCHHAUER,
BEVERLY W. BRANNAN, AND CLAUDINE WEATHERFORD

A lumbering boom swept the great wooded tracts of the East following the Civil War, denuding the southern Appalachians and much of the northern Great Lakes region. By the 1920s and 1930s, virtually all of the timber had been cut and most of the lumbermen had moved west. According to photographer Russell Lee, Minnesota's immense white pine forests were cut to serve the needs of the railroads. "It was beyond comprehension what they did up there," he said, "and there was no effort at conservation or anything like that."[1]

But the aftermath of logging was a matter of concern for the federal government's Resettlement Administration, a New Deal agency primarily responsible for improving the lot of the nation's farmers. The agency was particularly troubled by flooding along the Mississippi and its many tributaries, which reached a peak in the spring of 1937, and by the plight of farmers who occupied the cutover land. A major cause of the flooding was increased runoff from land stripped by logging, and the farm problem was particularly great for families who occupied land that had been logged. Such land has little productive value in any case, but the families' circumstances were made more difficult by northern Minnesota's short growing season and the generally depressed conditions of the 1930s.

The Resettlement Administration, renamed and expanded to become the Farm Security Administration during the very month most of the following photographs were made, carried on an active public relations program. Its Information Division contained a film unit headed by Pare Lorentz, whose well-known 1937 documentary *The River* described the floods and their causes and cried out for improved land use and conservation practices. The division also contained a still-photographic unit called the Historical Section. The section was headed by Roy Stryker and included such famous photographers as Dorothea Lange, Walker Evans, and Russell Lee.

The floods and the plight of farmers in the northern logging region were an important part of Russell Lee's first long-term photographic assignment. Lee joined the Historical Section in mid-1936, completed a couple of short trips and, in the autumn, began a Midwest trip that was planned for a matter of weeks but became a nine-month expedition. In February 1937, he photographed flooding on the Mississippi River; in April, May, and June, he trekked through northern Minnesota, Wisconsin, and Michigan; and in August and September he returned to the northern Great Lakes, where these pictures were made.[2]

There are a number of letters in Stryker's files concerning Lee's two visits to the region. Uppermost in the minds of the two men were the problems facing farmers on cutover land, some of whom were being resettled by the government, and Lee made many photographs of farmers in the area. Stryker always sought published outlets for his unit's photographs, and his letters to Lee refer to possible articles in *Scribner's* and *KEN* magazines and a book about the cutover lands.[3] In addition, Stryker was assembling photographs for a poem by Archibald MacLeish, and the work was published in 1938 in somewhat revised form under the ironic title *Land of the Free*.[4] This project gave Stryker a broad social frame for photographs from the region. "I am not sure how best to portray it," he wrote Lee in Michigan's Upper Peninsula, "but I wish that as you move across this area you would try to picture the remnants after the empire builders have finished,"[5] referring to copper and iron as well as timber.

It is impossible to see this series of pictures either as a statement about "the logging problem" or as an indictment of railroad-building robber barons. And, although the lumberjacks may have been underpaid and overworked, our present-day examination of Lee's empathetic photographs reveals only a group of hard-working and hard-playing men. The abstractions of Stryker's social concerns, rather than having been brought home by the particulars of Lee's photographs, have been lost to or absorbed within the humanity they depict. This contrasts with the effect of images like Dorothea Lange's famous Farm Security Administration photograph *Migrant Mother,* which tells us little about its subject, Florence Thompson, but is universally understood as signifying a failure of our society.

By 1937, the big operators had moved on, and Lee's subject is a relatively modest pulpwood outfit in Effie, Minnesota. The photographs portray the men moving logs out of the woods, performing various chores, preparing and eating food, bathing, and whiling away their leisure. Although this series does not show Lee at his most thorough, it does give evidence of his affection for describing processes and picturing detail. Stryker later referred to Lee as a taxonomist with a camera.[6] It is likely that the men joined Lee in identifying items to be documented; the sidelong glance in the picture of the dinner horn, for example, may indicate some collaboration between Lee and the cook in the making of the photograph.

When the pictures were filed at the agency, the photographs of the camp at Effie and most of the scenes from the nearby town of Craigville were placed in two different storage lots, an arrangement which probably reflects Lee's own separation of the subjects.[7] But five pictures filed with the Effie series lead us to think of the two subjects as one: a pair of stray pictures from the Craigville tavern and three photographs of the lumberjack with a bandaged eye. The captions for the pictures of the injured man inform us that he had been "beaten up and 'rolled' in a saloon in Craigville, Minn., on Saturday nite."[8] As if to bring home the point, the stray tavern shots were next in the file.

Lee, more than any member of Stryker's team, photographed life whole and as he found it. It is characteristic that Lee's coverage included the consumption of alcohol in its social setting, a subject eschewed by most of his colleagues. Some of the men share a bottle in the bunkhouse, while others are seen drinking and gambling in a nearby tavern. The content of the pictures is consistent with a September letter in which Lee wrote that he would be in Craigville for "pay-day in the lumber town."[9] Loggers were sometimes described in terms reserved for the Wild West; the 1938 Federal Writers Project guide to Minnesota describes nearby Bemidji (in its earlier heyday) as "one of the most lawless lumber centers in the Northwest."[10]

For Roy Stryker, the tavern was clearly part of a working man's life. Earlier in the year, he twice requested Lee to go to the notorious town of Hurley, Wisconsin—"see what you can get," he wrote, "and you'd better keep an eye on your virginity."[11] An April letter asks Lee to go to International Falls, Minnesota. "Not so many months ago [it] was one of the toughest towns on the border," Stryker wrote. "It is a meeting place of lumbermen, Indian traders, trappers, smugglers, immigration refugee smugglers, and so on. They used to kill a man every morning before breakfast and one just before supper, just for amusement."[12]

Although we cannot be completely certain that he was referring to this series, an October letter from Stryker praised a recent submission from Lee, saying, "The set on life in the lumber camp is tops."[13] The following week he wrote, "Your saloon pictures are superb," adding, "but I doubt if we are going to be able to use them as we have no releases from the people. Here is a problem, unfortunately, that we are going to have to work out."[14]

Photographic historians often use words like *humane* to describe the documentary images created by Russell Lee and the other photographers in Stryker's section. Often, this reflects an assessment of the team's deep concern about social issues and the way in which the photographs were used to define problems and to motivate attempts to solve them. This series shows that many of the photographs may also be characterized as *human;* they portray fully rounded human beings. It is easy to imagine a photographer assigned a story about logging who would limit his coverage to the work itself, and thus depict the men two-dimensionally, as workers. Lee's photographs show men as they actually lived—in the woods, at camp, and in town.

Photographs in Series

This series has been selected from the Farm Security Administration–Office of War Information (FSA–OWI) Collection in the Prints and Photographs Division of the Library of Congress, which contains about one hundred thousand photographs. The photographic unit which created the collection was formed within the Resettlement Administration in 1935. This agency became the Farm Security Administration in 1937. In 1942, the photographic section moved to the Office of War Information, where it continued its work until 1943, when Stryker resigned from the government.

The collection at the Library of Congress includes 107 photographs made at the camp near Effie, Minnesota, and in the nearby town of Craigville. Lee almost certainly exposed more film than this, but Stryker only kept the pictures he considered successful. We have selected twenty-one for presentation here. Lee never identified the camp or any of the men by name, but the letters, the contiguousness of the negatives, and the content of the pictures lead us to the conclusion that our selection represents a single logging operation.

At Effie, Lee did not photograph the first steps of the logging process: felling the trees and trimming and sectioning the logs. In his pictures, the process begins with the pulpwood being pulled out of the woods behind a caterpillar tractor or a team of horses. Other images show the logs being loaded onto railroad cars for transport to the mill. The notes which accompany the series do not explain whether the mixture of horses and machines is evidence of an operation in the throes of mechanization or one without the means to purchase much motorized equipment.

Some of the pictures were made with a Leica (negatives with an "M" suffix), a small, handy camera which offered as many as thirty-six exposures per roll of 35-mm film. Other pictures were made with a 3¼-by-4¼-inch Speed Graphic press camera (negatives with a "D" suffix). This camera was larger and clumsier, and the film packs which Lee used were limited to twelve exposures. But the Speed Graphic could be fitted with a flashgun, which Lee used for virtually all of the interior views in the series, and—as a rule—the larger negatives would be sharper than the small Leica negatives.

The August-September trip, as far as we can determine, was Lee's only venture with an 8-by-10-inch view camera. Its large sheets of film would yield exceedingly sharp images, but the camera was cumbersome and each setup was very time-consuming. Lee's experiment with it probably reflects the influence of his colleague Walker Evans, who favored the instrument, and Stryker's expressed desire for photographs which could be enlarged to mural size. We have included Lee's 8-by-10-inch photograph of Craigville's main street (negative with an "A" suffix). In a September letter to Lee, Stryker called the image "most excellent."

The FSA–OWI photographs have had a major impact on the history of documentary photography. Images from the collection regularly show up in publications and exhibitions, and certain photographs from the FSA period have become virtual icons of the Depression years. We are selecting a number of photographic series from the collection for a book and an exhibit at the Library of Congress which will mark the fiftieth anniversary of Stryker's photographic section.

The project's underlying concept is that a series of pictures conveys the variety and complexity of a subject more fully than a single image. A series' pictorial description can be further enriched by an accompanying text which delineates the circumstances of photography and characterizes the photographer's conception of the subject and working method. This approach to presenting FSA–OWI photographs contrasts with that taken by most of the recent books and exhibits that have drawn upon the collection. These have usually presented single images in a context which emphasizes the photographer's artistry and offer only the slightest reference to the subject matter or the era portrayed.

NOTES

1. Russell Lee, interview by Richard Doud, June 2, 1964. Archives of American Art, Washington, D.C.

2. Jack F. Hurley, *Portrait of a Decade* (Baton Rouge: Louisiana State University Press, 1972; New York: Da Capo, 1977); and Jack F. Hurley, *Russell Lee: Photographer* (Dobbs Ferry, N.Y.: Morgan and Morgan, 1978).

3. Roy Stryker to Russell Lee: January 30, April 3, April 10, ca. April 21, April 27, May 8, June 10, June 15, June 16, August 10, 1937, and other letters cited below. Roy E. Stryker Papers, University of Louisville Photographic Archives (hereafter cited as Stryker Papers; available on microfilm).

Lee to Stryker: March 20, April 28, May 2, 1937, Stryker Papers.

Lee to Edwin Locke: August 12, 1937, Stryker Papers.

Stryker to Leo Nicholas: January 15 and February 15, 1937, Box 2, Correspondence, General, 1937, FSA–OWI Textual Records, Prints and Photographs Division, Library of Congress (hereafter cited as FSA–OWI Textual Records; available on microfilm).

Stryker to Mrs. D. A. Levine, April 3, 1937, Box 2, Correspondence, General, 1937, FSA–OWI Textual Records.

4. Archibald MacLeish, *Land of the Free* (New York: Harcourt Brace, 1938).

5. Stryker to Lee: April 16, 1937, Stryker Papers.

6. Hurley, *Russell Lee: Photographer,* 14.

7. The photographs are from collection storage lots 1141 and 1143. At the Library, the actual photographic prints are kept in vertical files which are arranged by broadly conceived subject categories. In contrast, the microfilms of the original storage lots generally reflect the original assignments and shooting trips.

8. Caption for negative LC-USF33-11352-M3; FSA–OWI Collection, Library of Congress.

9. Lee to Locke: September 15, 1937, FSA–OWI Textual Records.

10. Federal Writers Project, *Minnesota: A State Guide* (1938; reprint New York: Hastings House, 1947).

11. Stryker to Lee: April 17, 1937, Stryker Papers.

12. Stryker to Lee: April 23, 1937, Stryker Papers.

13. Stryker to Lee: October 21, 1937, Stryker Papers.

14. Stryker to Lee: October 30, 1937, Stryker Papers.

In the Woods Near Effie, Minnesota

Stumps after cutting (LC-USF33-11355-M2)

*Caterpillar tractor skidding
logs through the woods
(LC-USF33-11356-M2)*

Crane operators loading logs onto rail cars (LC-USF34-30690-D)

Loaders pushing logs into place while loading a rail car (LC-USF33-11269-M3)

In Camp Near Effie, Minnesota

Log chains (LC-USF34-30674-D)

Left: Lumberjack with a stake that he has shaped with a broad axe. Some wood was prepared on site for use in sleds, buildings, and the like. (LC-USF33-11353-M2)

Below: Barn with stalls for horses (LC-USF34-30694-D)

Camp cook blowing the dinner horn (LC-USF33-11270-M4)

*Serving food (LC-USF34-
30677-D)*

Left: *Lumberjacks at dinner* (LC-USF34-30684-D)

Below: *Drying silverware* (LC-USF34-30686-D)

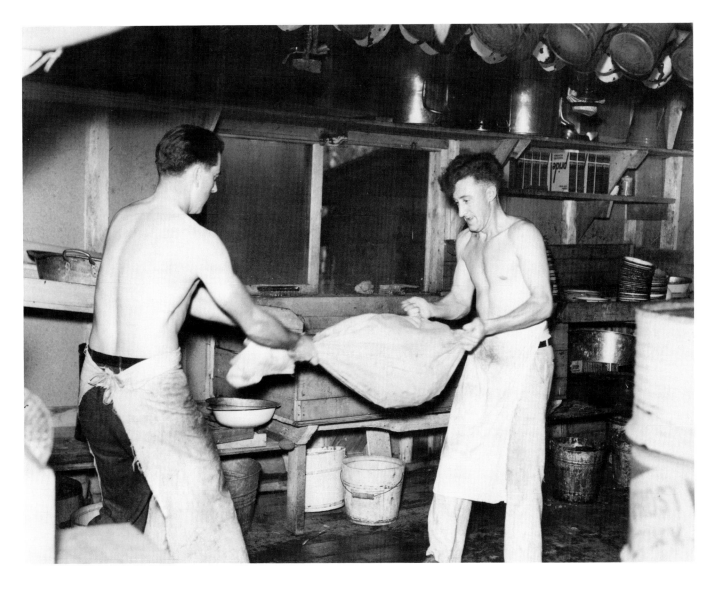

*Right: A lumberjack wash-
ing his feet (LC-USF34-
30689-D)*

*Below: Bath house (LC-
USF34-30697-D)*

Drinking in the bunkhouse
(LC-USF34-30691-D)

In camp. The men at right stage a mock fight for the camera; the man on the left told the photographer that his injury resulted from having been beaten and "rolled" in nearby Craigville on Saturday night. (LC-USF33-11352-M2)

Saturday in Craigville, Minnesota

View of the main street
(LC-USF342-30632-A)

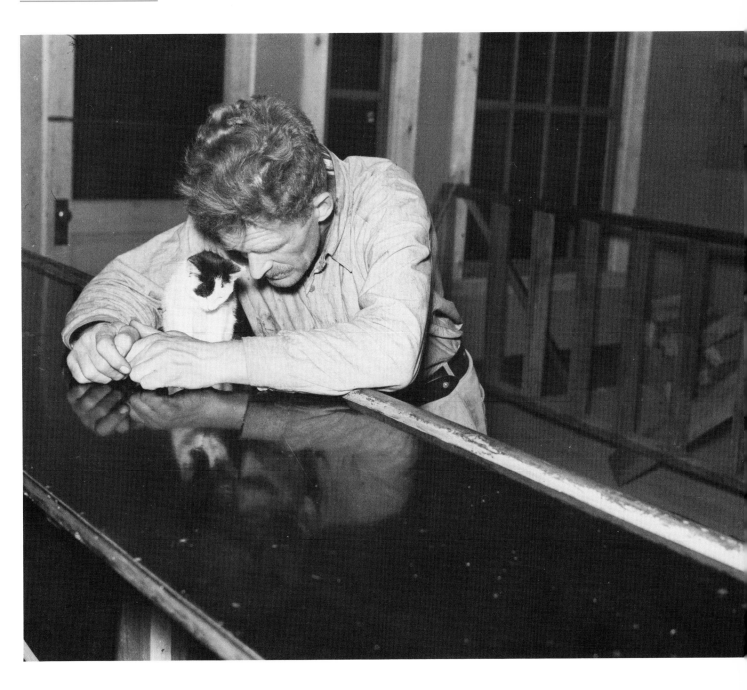

Via Dolorosa

BY ARVID ASPLUND

I heard the words "via dolorosa" for the first time about fifty years ago when they were used in a sermon preached by Pastor Walter Haase in St. John's Lutheran Church, Two Rivers, Wisconsin. Deeply impressed, I had a feeling of being linked to them, and I was inspired to write a hymn. The words constantly revisited my mind.

Perhaps it was the hardship of our early family life. Both of my parents were immigrants from Finland. In an effort to escape from adversities of their homeland, they came to America where they hoped to find better conditions. But it was a mirage. Their lives ebbed away before they reached their goals. My mother died from tuberculosis in 1914 at the age of twenty-eight. She left my father with two small children. In an effort to stabilize the family, he remarried a woman he did not know. The introduction occurred through a fellow workman who evidently thought it would help the family recover from misfortune. Unfortunately, my father's future path failed to improve. After many years of laboring in mines and quarries, lumbering, and farming, he died at the age of sixty-three.

My retirement in 1973 provided me with time to reflect upon my early family life. I had thought about writing a story for my children to read; and with this in mind, I approached the director at the Senior Center, Manitowoc, Wisconsin, concerning the possibility of creating a creative writing class. Several weeks later I was notified that Mr. Robert Gard, an author from the University of Wisconsin, Madison, was coming to Manitowoc to organize a class. Ten people, including myself, met with him, at which time he advised me to write about Finland.

A retired English teacher, Miss Agnese Dunne, volunteered to teach the class. We met with her at the Manitowoc Senior Center for one afternoon weekly for two years, and this is where my story developed. Because I felt that my early family life represented much sorrow, I entitled my story "Via Dolorosa."

Arvid Asplund, taken in 1977

This story is not strictly genealogical. Besides the tracing of my ancestors, it is a story of long family hardships. It is a story about Finnish immigrants who came to the United States in the early 1900s. The hardships they endured in the Old Country did not end as they had hoped in the United States. From antiquated farming in the Old Country, they immigrated into antiquated methods of mining iron ore in northern Michigan. Candles and carbide lights were then used to light the deep caverns below. Picks, shovels, and dynamite were used to loosen the iron rock from the earth's belly.

Miners' consumption, or tuberculosis, was a common disease that took many lives. At the age of twenty-eight my mother died of tuberculosis, evidently from poor living conditions. I was six years old at that time. My sister, Ethel, was two years old when our mother died. Later on, my father married again. This time to an illiterate Finnish woman. He hardly knew her but married her shortly after being introduced to her by a friend. Because she had previously worked in a lumber camp as a cook, the family moved up into the lumber woods. Most of my story is based on life in the wilds of northern Michigan.

The characters described in this book are not fictitious, and since they are all deceased, I'm using their real names.

I have never been to Finland, the home of my ancestors. However, I have gathered some facts about that country from a Finnish cookbook.

The territory comprises an area greater than Great Britain. It is as big as the states of Minnesota and Iowa combined. The population is thin—only four and one-half million people. It has the same latitudes as Alaska. One third of the area is north of the Arctic Circle. However, the ocean currents keep the country warm. The climate is much like the climate around the Great Lakes.

The sun rarely sets beyond the horizon. During the summer months they have daylight for twenty-two hours. It is known as the "land of the midnight sun."

Fifty thousand lakes glisten day and night. The country is bounded on the north by Norway, to the east by Russia, and to the west by Sweden. It is one of the Scandinavian group of countries. Russia ruled the country for one hundred years. Sweden ruled it previously for six hundred years.

The Finnish people are truly an ethnic people. There have been no immigrants to Finland in recent history. Their culture remains unadulterated.

The country is divided into fifteen provinces. One of these provinces, Karelia, was taken by the Russians during World War II. Four hundred and twenty thousand— the complete population of Karelia—became war refugees. They fled westward into Finland leaving all their possessions behind them. They were welcomed into the homes of the other Finns. The move was accomplished very smoothly, without any need for refugee camps. They lived in this manner until their resettlement could be worked out. Eventually all Karelians were given homes of their own. The Finns also gave of their money, jewelry, and any other valuable possessions to the Karelians. They harbored no enmity toward the Russians, feeling the act was due to their system of government.

The Finns are a nation of rugged individualists. They are a quiet, meditative people, noted for hard work and achievement. They excel individually—mostly in winter sports.

My father had purchased a piece of land in the early 1920s in northern Michigan. It consisted of forty acres of mostly wooded and untillable soil. It was located about two miles from a little village called Felch. I often walked to this land from the village with my father. We spent many long days cleaning away the stumps, stones, and brush, getting it ready for cultivation. I was about thirteen years old at that time. One day, during a rest period, I became rather inquisitive about my father's Scandinavian accent. "Where were you born, Pa?" I asked him. "Oh, so you vant to know ver I vas born? I vas born in Kvevlaks in Finland," he answered. "Farming vas tuff in Finland, too. I tink I find it better here," he said. Then I asked, "What made you think it would be better in America?" "Vel," he said, "Ve read newspapers in Finland about many good tings in America. All the young fellas in Finland say ve go to America to make big pay. Lots of gold mines, silver mines, and iron ore mines pay big. Potatoes grow big like watermelons and the land is cheap to buy. Lots of Finns come here because de vas starving in Finland and dey did not vant to fight in the Russian Army. I vas about twenty years old and got the fever to come to America." "How did you earn the money for the trip?" I asked him. "Oh, I could not make enough money for the trip in Finland, so I write to my friend, John Walsted, who vas in America before me. He vas vorking in a mine in Iron Mountain, Michigan. He tell me he vas making lots of money, and he send me the money to come to America." "Was it a nice trip?" I queried. "No, it vas not a good trip; it take us three veeks." "How come it took so long?" I asked. "Vel," he said, "Ve take train from Kvevlaks to Flango in Finland. Den ve go in small boat to Hull in England. From Hull ve take train to Southampton. Ve vait der for great big boat and den ve sail to New York." "Do you remember the name of the big boat?" I asked. "Ya," he answered. "It vas the VITE STAR. About two hundred Finns ver on dis boat, and de vas eating hardtack de bring vit them from home. Storm came and ve get a rough ride. Some people very sick. In dat time lots of sick people in Finland too. Finland vas in poor shape," he said. "What did you think of New York?" I asked. "Oh, ya, I vas fraid; I never before see so big place. Ve vas checked over like horses; den de put us on another train. Ven I get to Iron Mountain, Michigan, I meet my friend, John Walsted again. Den I vas happy," he said with a smile.

Years later while my wife and I were visiting the cemetery where my mother was buried, I met a man who I thought might be able to give me some information.

"Would you know if any of the Trewartha family is still alive?" I asked him.

"Sure," he said, "Bill Trewartha is still living. He's a bachelor and lives alone at Forbes Mining Location. If you would like to see him, I'll tell you how to get there."

After a few simple directions we left the cemetery and drove on a winding, uphill road to the Forbes location. We arrived and found it to be a small settlement of houses, but we did not know which house Bill lived in. A street repair crew, working nearby, provided the answer. As we drove over to his house, we found him polishing his car in his garage. He looked at us in bewilderment when we stopped across the street. I walked over to him and asked him, "Are you Bill Trewartha?" I could not identify him as the boy I used to know. I was looking at a white-haired old man.

"Yes," he responded. "And who are you?"

"I'm Arvid Asplund. I lived around here when I was a kid," I informed him.

"Well I'll be doggone," he retorted as he grabbed my hand and shook it vigorously. "I remember you," he went on. "You lived next door to us but your family moved away after your mother died. What is the purpose of your visit?"

I told him then about my recent retirement and that I intended to search for some family history and write a story about it, how I had come to see him because I wanted some information about the mining operations in this area, where my father had once worked.

"Well Arvid," he said, "I have been a bookkeeper all my life and have never been down in the mines, but Mr. Fredlund who lives around the corner should be able to give you all the information you want. His father was the captain in the mine your father worked in. He also has custody of a miner's museum. I'll call him on the phone; perhaps he'll be at home. Won't you come in while I call him?"

We accepted his invitation and sat down while he went over to the phone. I admired his spacious living room and everywhere I looked there was evidence of good housekeeping. Unusual, I thought, for a bachelor.

He returned from the phone and said, "Mr. Fredlund will be here in a few min-

utes." While we were waiting for him we began talking about the old Davidson location where we had once lived. The cluster of homes near a mine was called a location.

"Is the Davidson location still there?" I asked. "If so, I would like to visit my old home."

"No," he said. "All the old homes have been moved out. The land around them began to cave in. It became a dangerous place to live. This house was moved here from Davidson. The one you lived in is now across the street from mine."

"Will you show me which one was ours?" I asked eagerly. "I'd like to take a picture of it."

We stepped outside on his back porch and he pointed it out to me. It seemed to be in good shape, I thought, but I could not relate to it because it had been remodeled. The open front porch that our hired girl sat on with her boyfriend on balmy summer evenings was gone. (An old thought flashed back. I remembered how I enjoyed spying on her when she thought I was asleep inside.) I walked around the house snapping a few pictures. Then I took a picture of old Bill Trewartha standing on his back porch.

Mr. Fredlund then arrived and said he would take us to the Miner's Museum. It was located about two miles out from Iron River, Michigan. He showed us a replica of an iron ore mine. It was a model showing the surface buildings, the shaft, the engine house, and the workings underground. He flipped a switch and the mine was flooded with light. Miniature machinery began to operate in the depths below the surface. An ancient picture came back to my mind. I could see some men with my father being lowered into the mine in a cage. They were dressed in oilskin clothing to protect them from the dripping water below. Carbide lamps were attached to the fronts of their oilskin hats. Down, down, down they went, one thousand feet into the belly of the earth. Then the cage would stop and the men filed out, one by one. Silly silhouettes marched along the walls of the tunnel as the men walked forward. The flickering flame from their carbide lights magnified the determination on their faces. Coming to a large excavation at the end of the tunnel, they

picked up some tools and began to toil with picks, shovels, drills, and hammers. They drilled holes into the iron rock like human moles. This rock was dynamited loose and hoisted to the surface in chunks. It was later melted into iron and used to industrialize the New World. This was the world these men had strived to reach. They were young and vigorous men. Their eyes sparkled with hope, although the burden of this world was on their backs.

Such was the beginning of my father's life in this country.

Across the road from our house at Felch, Michigan, lived an old Finnish couple in a log home. Several hundred feet away from their home stood another smaller log hut. I often wondered what the hut was used for. I became extremely inquisitive one day when I saw them carrying wood and branches into this hut. I asked my father, "What are they doing in that hut?"

"Oh," he said, "Dey is getting ready for a bat. Dat is de kind of bat dey have in Finland. Old man Coypaleen he get dat idea from de people in Finland. Every farmer in Finland have a building like dat vun. Sometimes dey build dem by a lake ver de vater is handy."

"Do they have a bathtub in there?" I asked him.

"No," he said, "only a vooden tub made from a hollow log. It is filled vit cold water."

"Do they take a bath in cold water?" I went on.

"No, dey make hot steam in der. First dey make hot fires in da stove. Dey have stones on top of stove and dey get hot, too. Ven it get so hot in der, dey take off all clothes and de svet come out like dew drops. Den dey have some birch branches dey put in de vater. Dey sprinkle dis vater on de hot stones and da room is filled vit steam. Den dey dip de birch branches in de vater again and splash der bodies vit dem. Dey rub some soap on and do dis again. Den dey sit on de bench by de vall to get cool. Some tuff Finns yump in de lake to cool off. Dey tink it vill make them helty. In de vintertime dees tuff Finns yump in the snow. Do you tink you could do dat?"

"No," I answered, "when I jump in the snow I want to have my boots on."

In the early 1900s, miles of boardwalks lined the streets of Iron Mountain, Michigan. It was customary for the local gallant swains to stroll along these walks on Sunday afternoons. Not that these sports were "in need of exercise"—they got plenty of that in the mines, but they were hoping to meet the lassies who were eager to flirt with them.

It was in this manner that my father met my mother. A friend introduced her to him on the boardwalk. Her name was Mary Herrgard. Mary was also an immigrant from Finland, speaking the Swedish language. She had some relatives in Iron Mountain who had arranged for her passage to this country. She and father were both young and felt lonely in a new world. After a few months of courtship, they decided to enter wedlock. She was twenty-one and he was twenty-two years old. The marriage certificate at the courthouse in Iron Mountain gives the date, August 19, 1907. It was signed by John E. Quarnstrom, who was the county clerk at that time. Mary gave her father's name as Abraham Herrgard. For some mysterious reason, she did not know her mother's name. My father listed his father's name as John Svarven, his mother's as Tilda Svarven. It was customary for immigrants at that time to change their names when they arrived in this country. My father took the name of Asplund, probably because he knew some nobleman by that name in Finland. In Swedish the name means "Poplar Grove."

The wedding ceremony was held in the Saron Lutheran Church at Fourth and Vulcan Streets in Iron Mountain, Michigan. The clergyman was the Reverend Carl Almen. Oscar and Mathilda Shoberg attended the bride and groom.

A strange course for the two young people was set on this day.

Courthouse records at Iron Mountain, Michigan, indicate that I was born there on March 14, 1908. I do not recollect any of my childhood in that city. I do remember starting school in Stambaugh, Michigan. It was a huge red brick building at the east end of Main Street. Entering that big build-ing alone terrified me the first day. I felt like making a stampede for home. I can recall no schoolmates. The teacher was very kind to me.

My school days in Stambaugh were cut short when we moved to the Davidson Mining Location in Iron River, Michigan. Here the days were more pleasant. I had some neighbor kids to go to school with me. The location was made up of about ten average-looking homes where the miners lived. The superintendent of the mine, Rudolph Erickson, lived at the end of the street in a more attractive home.

The Davidson Mine was nearby and a trail through the woods led to the James School. This school opened in November 1913. The principal was Miss Margaret Flanagan. A family of Italians lived across the road from us. They had two pretty girls about my age, also a group of very noisy boarders. I enjoyed walking to school with these two girls.

The boarders at the girls' home played a clamorous, shouting game on their off-time called Bo-Chee, a bowling type of game, played with large hardwood balls and one small ball. It was played on a cinder-packed court in the yard. A small ball was placed in the distance. The object seemed to be to strike the small ball by rolling a large ball toward it. It was a typical Italian game.

These boarders were a very thirsty bunch. They drank wine avidly during the game. The more they drank, the louder their laughter and the higher their shouts rang out. The beverage that fired their enthusiasm was called "Dago-Red," a homemade very sour wine made from grapes. I can remember seeing these grapes come in by the truckload to the home.

There were other sights to see at the boarding house. Rows of bread dough in loaves were laid on boards near the ceiling. The warmth up there helped the dough rise, ready for baking.

A long dinner table was needed to accommodate all the boarders. A bottle stood

by each plate. Wine and beer was served with every meal.

The evening chore for little girls was to tap beer from large kegs into quart bottles. I watched them do this in their cellar many times. I was very fond of these two girls and enjoyed their company.

Later on a neighbor boy next door to us joined the scene. On wintry nights we would take a gunny sack over to the engine house at the mine. In the dark, we would fill it with coal. Then we carried it over to the girls' house and were treated with a bottle of beer. I was eight or nine years old at this time.

On our trip over to the mine at night, we discovered a window opened about three inches at the bottom for ventilation. A package of tobacco usually rested inside the sill. When the engineer wasn't looking, we'd sneak up under the window and steal some of his tobacco. We would put the package back in place, and he never seemed to catch on.

The first time I smoked tobacco, I became very ill. Coming home pale and vomiting, my parents thought I had contracted a serious disease. Eventually they discovered tobacco in my back pocket. My father tried to cure me with spanking, but it didn't work. Tobacco intrigued me. I gradually became accustomed to it.

Another of our exciting pastimes was collecting empty carbide cans from the mine. A residue of carbide was usually left in the bottom of these cans. By adding water to this carbide, it would create a form of gas. Quietly we would hammer down the cover and scamper away to a safe distance. When the gas inside built up enough pressure, it blew the cover off in a striking explosion.

What dangerous fun we had.

His tombstone reads, "John Trewartha, born 1904, died 1967." I knew John well as a child. His family lived next door to mine. His mother immigrated from Cornwall County in England. His father came from Rhodesian ancestors; however,

he was born in New Jersey. We called my playmate Jack. He and I played around the local mine looking for excitement.

When the big, black locomotive switched iron ore cars around, we were there to hitch a ride. The step at the rear of the locomotive was our favorite stand. We would jump on when the train was moving slowly, and then jump off as it picked up speed. I can't remember ever being caught by the engineer; perhaps he saw us but didn't want to spoil our fun.

Chipmunks were plentiful around the mines. They played games with us in the piles of logs and rocks. The little rascals would sit on their haunches and make faces at us. When we threw a stone at them, they would dart into a hole, scamper back in a few seconds, and resume their antics. Jack searched the brush nearby and made some thin poles. We pulled a few long black strands of hair from the tail of a grazing horse. We improvised long snares with this strong hair and tied them to one end of our poles. This contraption proved to be an excellent trap. Slowly we moved our snares over the heads of the chipmunks. They seemed to be blind to the black snare. When we had it circled around their heads, we raised the pole with a quick jerk. The chipmunk was caught like a fish.

Carving whistles from branches that had soft bark was another trick I learned from Jack. Our favorite source of whistle wood was the rubber tree. By hammering the bark with the handle of a knife, it would slide off quite easily.

Summer afternoons were usually spent at the swimming hole. It was a sunny spot in the woods where a little lazy creek meandered. We had no bathing suits. On one occasion, some little girls surprised us with a visit. Nude and red-faced, we scampered to shore for our clothes. Hurriedly I pulled on my knickers and slipped into my shirt. I felt a sharp sting on my back, another, and then another. I screamed at the top of my lungs. I ripped off my shirt and saw a bee fly out. To this day I am deathly afraid of bees.

Three children were given life by my mother before she passed away. I was the first, born on March 14, 1908. A brother,

Albert, was born in 1910. He died three years later from spinal meningitis. Sister, Ethel, was born May 10, 1912.

We were living at the Davidson Mining Location in Iron River, Michigan, when my mother died; the year was 1914. I was six years old, and my sister was two years old. I remember very little about my mother or any attention she must have given me. Who taught me the little Swedish prayer that I still recite? Perhaps it was my mother. My only vision of my mother was that she was bedridden. She had tuberculosis.

Mr. and Mrs. Sundquist, friends of my father, came to help out with the family. A premonition must have come over Mrs. Sundquist one morning as she got me ready for school. "Why don't you say good-bye to your mother?" she asked me. I went to her bedside. She looked very ill; with some effort she stretched out her arm and clasped my hand in hers. It was cold and damp. "Good-bye, Arvid," she whispered. I then ran off to school. Arriving home that afternoon, a veil of black crepe was hanging on our door. My mother died at the age of twenty-eight.

After that tragedy, many different people came to visit our house. Mr. and Mrs. Oscar Shoberg came, and he would bring his violin. He said he was going to teach me how to play his violin, but we never reached that point. He became an attraction playing in the saloons downtown. He often mentioned being at Piccolino's Saloon in Stambaugh.

Once after a day of cold and heavy rainfall, I went out barefooted to play in the water. A sore throat and an earache beset me that night. The infection in my tonsils made them so large I could not swallow food. My ear ached so much I cried and could not sleep. An old miner who smoked a corncob pipe was visiting with my father. He came to my bedside and blew smoke into my ear. It affected me like an anesthetic. My pain went away and I fell asleep. The next day a doctor came to see me. He looked me over and said, "That boy has scarlet fever." The house was quarantined for several weeks thereafter. This siege of scarlet fever left me with a perforated eardrum that bothered me intermittently for many years.

A paternal uncle arrived in this country from Finland in 1909. He was a tailor by trade. Werner was his first name and he adopted the last name of Smith. Being a good cook besides being a tailor, he was a great help in our household. In 1914 after my mother died, he decided to take me with him back to Finland. However, World War I broke out, and he had to change his plans. Germany was sinking our ships at sea, and it was too dangerous to be out in the ocean.

My uncle Werner proved to be my best benefactor. No one ever gave me so much affection and attention. He bought clothing for me and things with which to play. I promptly got into trouble with a "BB" gun he bought for me. He took me to a photographer, and we had our picture taken (I standing in front of him). Werner was a bachelor at that time, a teetotaler and a very religious man. He stood out like a saint in that rough and tough mining settlement. I came to respect him and revered him the rest of his life. I can still picture him kneeling at my bedside praying.

It was a black day for me when he left us to work at the Stolberg Tailor Shop in Iron Mountain, Michigan. After that parting, I saw very little of my good uncle, Werner Smith.

A young hired girl came to help in our household. She had a boyfriend, and I was in their way. My father was working on the night shift. Her boyfriend took her to a carnival one night, and I had to tag along. She gave me some money and said, "Go and ride on the Merry-Go-Round." When I had used all my tickets, I had to get off the ride. I looked around for her, but she was nowhere in sight. She and her boyfriend had disappeared. It was dark. I didn't know the way back home. I was being pushed around by crowds of people. The strange faces and the excitement around the carnival filled me with horror. I began to cry, and I cried and cried. Finally some people asked, "Are you lost, little boy?" I said,

"Yes, I don't know how to get back to the Davidson Location." "Come with us, we'll take you home," the lady said. Now I felt safe. I had met some good Samaritans.

It was 1917, the war was over, but another fight was just beginning for me. My father had been away for several days on a mysterious mission. A large, heavy-set woman accompanied him on his return. "Is she going to be our new hired girl?" I asked. "No," he said, "Dis is your new mudder." I looked her over suspiciously. She had a large stomach, and I thought she looked mean.

This match had been arranged by a friend of my father's who knew my stepmother. Evidently my father thought this marriage would solve his family predicament. The first few days were uneventful.

A big boy arrived at our house a few days later, and he was about five years my senior.

One day while playing around the mine, a man called to me and said, "Hey kid, how would you like to have a puppy?"

"What kind of a puppy?" I asked him.

"An English bulldog," he said, "I have four of them, and if you come over to my house tonight you can have your pick."

I was delighted and that night I hurried over to his house to look at the puppies. One of them was pure white. I decided to take him home with me. I was sure he would grow up to be a champ.

He was not destined to live very long.

A few days later, I came home from school to find my puppy floating in a tub of water in our backyard. My stepmother assured me that the dog jumped into the water and drowned, but I had some misgivings about the incident. With a heavy heart, I buried my prize in the backyard.

Blood Bread became my next curiosity.

My stepmother said she wanted to make some blood bread, but she would need some fresh blood. My father told her about a slaughterhouse in town where fresh blood might be available. The next day she and I, each carrying an empty pail, set out for the slaughterhouse. She could speak no English so I had to tell the men that she wanted some blood. They looked at me with this big lady and began to laugh.

"What are you going to do with the blood?" they asked. "To make blood bread," I answered.

We watched them kill a cow by hitting her on the head with a hammer. The cow fell down and they slit her throat with a knife. The blood gushed out. They took our pails and held them under her neck. Soon they were full of blood and we set out for home with our bloody booty.

My stepmother mixed this blood into some bread dough, formed it into flat, round loaves, and baked it without pans in the oven. When finished and sliced, it was a very dark brown bread. We ate a lot of this bread in the years that followed.

My stepmother had previously been a cook in the lumber camps in northern Michigan. So with the arrival of fall, a man by the name of Matt Blomquist came to our house. He was setting up a lumber camp and she had to take over this duty. Her son was to be the choreboy and my father would work in the woods cutting logs.

Our meager household goods were sold, and we prepared to move into the timber country. We made the trip from Iron River to Metropolitan, Michigan, by auto. Then we transferred to a supply wagon pulled by a team of heavy horses. After what seemed like hours of plodding, we arrived at the camp, late in the afternoon. It consisted of two long log cabins end to end. A breezeway in between the cabins was filled with firewood. One cabin was called the men's shack. The other one was called the cook shack. We unloaded our supplies and set up our beds in the cook shack.

There was no schooling for me that winter. I had left the fourth grade behind me at the James School in Iron River. One memento I have saved—it is a Certificate Award for not being absent or tardy in 1915, signed by Myrtle L. Champion. She was my second grade teacher, and a vision of her beauty still lingers in my memory.

The first day at the camp was spent in exploration. There was a barn made of logs for the horses; a couple of hogs in a pen nearby; and an outdoor privy and a creek from which we carried water. This scene became my lonely playground for the next several months. At nightfall I would crawl under the blankets and cry softly until the sandman carried me away.

I would be awakened before daybreak to help set the table for breakfast. Fifteen men came in to eat at the sound of a gong. They devoured flapjacks, sausages, and coffee, and then set out for work. These were strong men who worked with crosscut saws, axes, and cant hooks. After they left for work, Andrew and I would do the chores, carry in fresh supplies of firewood and water, sweep out the men's shack, and clean the lamp chimneys, help do the dishes, and then clean out the barn and feed the hogs. Andrew would often find an excuse to leave the camp and go to town. Then I would be left to do the chores alone.

The bunks in the men's shack were made from boards covered with straw. A woolen blanket covered the straw and two extra blankets were used to cover them while they slept. The tidiness of these bunks was left to whoever occupied them. A large black iron stove squatted in the center of the shack. It had wooden racks on each side. The men used these racks to dry their heavy woolen socks or anything else that was wet. Sometimes they brought in horse collars to dry. A strong odor pervaded the men's shack from these socks. Laundering was done on Sundays, since each had to do his own. Some men neglected this duty. Water had to be heated in an iron pot over an outdoor fire. Each man had a gunny sack for his personal effects. This gunny sack also served as a pillow at night.

Tobacco was used by most of the lumberjacks. Some of them used snuff. I had to try it. During the day, when the men were away at work, I would explore the stuff on the shelves in the bunks. Finding a box of snuff, I would take a pinch and put it inside my lip. This became a daily habit. Before the winter was over, I was a steady snuff

chewer and could spit between my teeth. A box of snuff became my steady companion.

Logs had to be hauled out of the woods on roads built up with ice when the cold weather season came. This was done by hauling large tanks of water over the roads and flooding them with water at night. The icy roads enabled a team of horses to pull a load of logs out of the woods to a place they called the landing. The sleds loaded with logs would gain too much speed when going downhill. When the horses had difficulty controlling the loads, sand was thrown in the ruts, ahead of the advancing load of logs. The man who did this was called the sandhill man. His work was to prevent the load of logs from crushing the horses that pulled it.

Hauling all the logs out of the woods before the ice melted was a constant struggle. The roads were repeatedly watered at night to keep them hard and slippery. When spring finally arrived the camp broke up, and we moved into a little village called Felch, Michigan. It was 1918, and I had reached my tenth birthday.

In the spring of 1918, we migrated from Blomquist's Lumber Camp to Felch, Michigan. A narrow, graveled road ran through the village. Most of the homes dozed on their way to degeneration. The nearest doctor, dentist, or barber was twenty-five miles away at Iron Mountain, Michigan. This was the village my stepmother had lived in before she joined my father.

It was a quiet village of about a hundred Scandinavian immigrants. These people made their living mostly from the lumbering business. The male element worked in the tall timber during the late fall and winter months. In the spring and summer, they sought jobs on road construction and usually had some cattle and a little land which brought in some food. There was very little sign of life in the village except around the stores. One store was called the Felch Supply Company, which got its name from its function to the lumber camps. The other store was Ryan's, and they also ran the post office in their establishment.

On lazy summer days, it was a common sight to see a group of men and boys lounging in front of Ryan's Store. They would be swapping tales and telling jokes while waiting for the arrival of the daily mail. After that event, they would disperse, vanishing like thin smoke.

The mail came in daily by train. However, the train also came in for other reasons. There were loads of logs to be pulled out and occasionally a load of stone from a local quarry. The high point of a dull day would be to wait down by the depot and watch the train come chugging in.

A deserted saloon and three dance halls increased the town's image. An old tale was repeated about a man who was killed in that saloon, and how the owner had fled to Canada. Ryan's had a dance hall above the garage across the road from their store and country hotel. Another hall was known as the Runeberg Hall. It was owned by the local Runeberg Society. I don't remember the name of the third dance hall. All of these buildings were of the wood-frame type on wood post foundations. These dark and gloomy halls were vacant most of the time. Occasions did occur when one or the other would burst into life with some local function. Accordions and concertinas were the favorite instruments for the dances. My ears still ring with the concertina music played by Caviani from Iron Mountain, Michigan.

A little ice cream store snuggled near one of these dance halls. It was opened on weekends by the Matt Backlund family.

The most distinctive building in town was the two-story, red brick township school. All twelve grades were taught in this school by 1929. A Sunday School class also used this building. A kindly gentleman by the name of John Sundstrom was the principal-teacher. He also owned the local garage. A portly young lady named Miss Minnie Ryan was his assistant on Sundays.

This was my hometown for the next nine years. The first house we lived in was owned by the Felch Supply Company. It was a well-built house and had a kitchen, dining room, and two bedrooms on the first floor. The attic remained unfinished except for the floor. The house was located on a half acre of land, surrounded by a variety of trees, and an abundance of wild flowers. Our water was pumped up from a well. A hog pen, small barn, a privy, and a woodpile also made up the scene.

For those who looked at us from the outside, it must have seemed an idyllic home, but for those on the inside, it was a churning volcano.

"Get out of my way, you tubercular bum. Put that book away and get the barn cleaned out." She slapped me and grabbed my book. I had been reading it by the light of the oil lamp near the stove. This was my stepmother's way of greeting me in the morning.

The winter mornings were dark and cold. My duty was to be the first to rise and start the fire in the kitchen stove. The oil lamp hung in a bracket on the wall near the stove. I would stand up and read by this lamp until the rest of the family awakened.

My father would be away at work in some lumber camp and came home only for the weekends. My stepbrother had a job in the village. He worked on the railroad as a section hand.

I would leave the house and out to the barn I would go. There I shoveled manure, and fed the cows with hay and middling. The mice in the barn would sneak over to the sack of middling for their breakfast. I would stand still and watch until I saw some movement in the sack. Then I would raise my shovel high and with one quick blow I would exterminate one mouse. Then back to the house I would run to get my breakfast and some more tongue lashing.

"Here, eat this, you tubercular bums."

It was my stepmother again, growling at us while she was setting the table. Our usual breakfast was a bowl of cultured milk with a slice of blood bread. Our two cows kept us supplied with plenty of milk. I often churned the cream by hand into butter.

"Come along with me to the barn, you

tubercular bum. You can hold the cow's tail for me while I do the milking." My stepmother would shout in Swedish. She spoke no English.

"You . . . get those dishes washed before you go to school." That command went to my sister, Ethel, who was about seven years old.

In the barn, I would stand by, holding the cow's tail to keep it from switching on my stepmother's face while she was milking. Back to the house we went with the milk. My little sister, Ethel, had the table clean and had washed the dishes.

A few reminders of my father's first marriage were stored away in the attic in our house at Felch. There were some pictures, books, and some jewelry. One day my sister, Ethel, was helping my stepmother clean up the attic. A Swedish Bible lay in with some other books. My stepmother opened it and saw some handwriting inside the cover. She asked Ethel to read it. It read, "To my little daughter, Ethel, may God be with you always."

"Your mother died from tuberculosis," my stepmother said. "That book is filled with germs; take it downstairs and throw it in the fire."

Downcast, Ethel took the Bible downstairs. She opened the lid on the kitchen stove and pretended she had thrown it in. Then she took the Bible and hid it under her bed. Later on she moved it to a different hiding place. She still has the Bible to this day.

My father had saved a little money from his job in the lumber woods during the winter of 1918. That spring he decided to buy a piece of land about one mile from the village. His plan was to develop this land into a farm and build a home on it. It covered forty acres, with about one acre cleared for cultivation. One half of the land was a tamarack swamp. The remainder was covered with brush and stumps. The tamaracks proved to be a good source for firewood, which we used for both cooking and heating in our home. We spent many hours with an axe and a saw to provide enough wood for the winter months. We had to hire someone with horses to pull it home for us.

We also hired a team of horses to help clear our land of stumps, logs, and rocks. The rocks were hauled to the edges of the field on a stone boat. There we piled them up along the fence line. Brush, stumps, and other debris were piled up and set on fire.

As a young boy, I worked with my father on this land. He was a very tough and determined worker. He was thin and of medium height. When his hands were free, he walked straight as a stick. We carried food along out to the land for our lunch at noon. After our lunch, my father would stretch out on the grass, lie flat on his back, and close his eyes.

"Better days are coming," he would sigh.

I can recall driving the horses while he would guide the plow. The land was very stony, and he would get a jolt whenever the plow hit a rock. We managed to clear about four acres with a lot of perspiration and frustration. Finally we had it ready for cultivation. We planted potatoes and the grain was sown by hand. The soil was rich, and the crops flourished. When the time came for the harvest, the grain was cut with a horse-drawn mower. Then it was raked into bunches, tied into bundles, and shocked. My father taught me how to do the shocking. The trick was to pile the bundles on end, and lean them against each other in the shape of a wigwam. The tops had to face the sun so that the grain would ripen.

Making the shocks stand up was a disappointing experience for me. I would dream about this at night. One night I had a nightmare, got up, and began shocking grain in my sleep.

One threshing machine served all the local farmers, and we helped each other thresh. I went over to help our neighbor, big John Mattson, with his threshing. At the end of the day he said, "Arvid, you handle those bags of grain just like a man. I'm going to pay you a man's wages." He made me feel important. Our soil was rich and our crops were bountiful. Besides potatoes and grain, we grew red clover and alfalfa hay. We built a protective cover for our hay. It was nothing more than a roof made with boards and supported with posts and braces.

I helped my father to plant a little orchard on our land. We had about a dozen apple trees and a few plum trees.

There was no time for play during our school vacations. We were busy every day raising food in some way. My sister and I picked a lot of berries. Raspberries and blueberries were easy to find in that area. Many berries missed the pail by being tossed into our mouths. Most of the families in the village had a cow or two. These cows were allowed to roam at will. They were not fenced in. Each cow had a bell around its neck so that we could find them at milking time. We had a cow that seemed to be a leader. Other cows would follow her wherever she would go. She loved to eat wild onion and would go deep into the woods searching for it. When this happened, it was hard to find where the cows had gone. That's when the bells came into play. I developed an ear for music trying to locate our cowbell. I would listen intently for a tinkling sound somewhere in the distance. Often I found they had strayed far away from the quiet village. After many cow-hunting trials, I learned to distinguish our bell, even when it was mixed with many other bells.

Once in the early morning, and then again in the evening, a young, barefoot boy in tattered overalls could be seen bringing a herd of cows into the village.

Rain or shine, I was that boy.

Although I missed the fourth grade by being in the lumber camp, I was placed in the fifth grade with the other kids my age in the Felch Township School.

Miss Novak was my teacher throughout the fifth and sixth grades. Besides teaching us the three R's, she taught us manual training. There were no male teachers at that time. It was an amusing sight to see Miss Novak sawing and planing boards, but she did teach us how to make things from wood. She also taught a course in agriculture. I seemed to excel in this course. Helping my father on our farm and my daily job of getting the cows seemed to help me with this study. As a result of my good marks, I won a trip to the Michigan State Fair at Detroit. The trip was sponsored by the county to the three boys with the highest grades. The County Agricultural Agent was our escort. We left Iron Mountain, Michigan, by train in a sleeping car. The drawing room was assigned to us. This was a private room, accommodating several people in one end of the car.

Three days were spent at the fair viewing all the shows and exhibitions. On the fourth day we left for home in a new Model T Ford. The County Agent bought this car while we were in Detroit and drove us back home in it. I can remember passing through Manitowoc on our way home. We stopped at a restaurant on Eighth Street for a lunch. While we were eating we saw a young man dash out of the restaurant without paying his bill.

School did have some exciting moments. During recess time, we played a game called scheeney. It was a game similar to hockey but played without skates. To prepare for this game, each boy had to have a club with a hook on the lower end. A nearby woods provided us with these clubs. By cutting the sticks off below the ground along the roots, we found the desired hook for our clubs. A tin can was used in place of a puck. In the process of a hard hitting game, this can would be hammered into a ball shaped puck. It was not unusual for someone to be injured when struck by a club or by this flying can.

In the wintertime, we often had to start our game on a field of fresh snow. After playing for some time, the snow would be packed into a hard surface.

Another picture of my school days lingers in my mind. A girl with pitch black hair sat in front of me in school. I could see the head lice crawling around in it. Sometimes a louse would fall off her head onto my desk. I would crush it with my pen. Bathing facilities did not exist in our home nor in the homes of my schoolmates. Swimming in the summertime was the only way we had a chance to bathe.

I began to feel very ill in school one morning. Miss Novak noticed my discomfort and came over to my desk and said, "Arvid, you better go home. I can see you are getting the measles."

I was glad to be excused and sadly dragged myself home. My stepmother was standing on the back porch near a rain barrel.

"What's the matter with you?" she asked in an angry voice.

"I'm sick and I want to go to bed," I replied.

"Hand me that empty pail by the pump," she commanded with a sly look.

I got the pail and passed it up to her on the porch. Quickly she dipped the pail into the barrel, pulled it out, and dumped the water over me. She said nothing more, but her eyes blazed with hatred. I dawdled into the house, undressed, and tumbled into bed.

Can you imagine me being a member of a notorious gang? Well here is how it happened.

Albin Hegman, a classmate of mine, aspired to become a leader. He was our "idea" man.

"Let's organize a gang," he said. "There are seven of us, so we'll call our gang the Silent Seven."

"Where can we meet?" I asked him.

"We'll meet in the old pool hall," he said. "Harold Solberg has a key that fits the back door. We'll meet there tonight."

The pool hall was an abandoned saloon with two pool tables in it. The front door had a large padlock on it, but the back door could be opened with a skeleton key. We got together and sneaked in at dusk. There were no lights in the old saloon. Our meeting was a very spooky affair. We must have frightened the rats out of the building.

Albin was elected president. I became the treasurer. It was my duty to collect five cents per week from each member. In due time our treasury swelled to several dollars. We decided we ought to have some appropriate pins to designate our membership. Albin answered an ad in a magazine and got a catalog of pins showing various colors and designs. We made a selection and soon we were sporting some fancy pins with the inscription, "S.S."

"What does that mean?" the kids would ask us.

"It means we belong to the Silent Seven," we would tell them. "It's a very secret organization."

Our gang holed up in the old saloon and whiled away many hours shooting pool.

A group of the local girls got their heads together and cooked up an idea to use the Silent Seven for some entertainment. Esther Lindstrom was the spokesman for the girls. She approached Albin and said, "We girls would like to go for a hayride with the Silent Seven." We discussed the possibilities at our next meeting. One of the boys, George Wickman, said, "I'll ask my dad for the horses and a rack full of hay." By the following Saturday night we were all set for the ride. When the girls arrived, George asked Esther, "Where do you want to go?"

"Let's go to Foster City," she answered. "Foster is only five miles from here. We can have some ice cream and pop there and then we'll come back."

"Okay," we said, and we set off with the horses on a trot. We had a good time for a while singing songs like "Oh! What a Pal was Mary," "The Old Gray Mare," "It Ain't Gonna Rain No More," and "Barney Google."

When we arrived at Foster City, we pulled up in front of the ice cream parlor. A gang of boys came out to meet us. They were very friendly with our girls, and it soon became evident that they had been expecting this visit. The girls climbed out of the hay rack, paired up with the boys and vanished into the darkness. Surprised at this turn of events, rejected and dejected, we turned the horses around and headed for home.

Now we were . . . a very Silent Seven.

Members at that time were: Albin Hegman, Axel Hegman, Harold Solberg, Pally Solberg, Arvid Asplund, Wally Brandstrom, and George Wickman.

The Zion Lutheran Church was the only established church near our home. The membership was all of Scandinavian descent, and the services were held in the

Swedish language. Although my father was not able to give any financial support to this church, he did urge me to become a Lutheran.

The summer of 1923 was spent going to confirmation school. We had to study and memorize the Swedish catechism. My confirmation took place on October 14, 1923. A Swedish Bible was given to me at that time. It was signed by the Reverend G. A. Ostergren, and my memory verse was from the first book of Corinthians, chapter 1, paragraph 30:

But of Him are ye in Christ Jesus, who of God is made unto us wisdom, and righteousness and sanctification and redemption.

The pages of my Swedish Bible have turned yellow with age.

With grammar school and confirmation behind me, I decided to try to earn my own living. At home my sister and I were being tongue-lashed and buffeted constantly by my stepmother. The house had become crowded by two new additions to the family. I was anxious to get out. I learned about a man who was building a new lumber camp, and I went to see him.

"Do you need a chore boy for your new camp?" I asked him.

"Yes, I do need a chore boy," he said. "But you are too young; you should go back to school."

"I don't want to go back to school; I want to earn some money," I answered.

"Well," he said, "I'll talk to your father about it."

A few days later my dad told me John Mattson talked to him and said he would like to have me as a chore boy for his camp.

"Can I go?" I asked him.

"Yes," he said, "You can go. You will get lots of good food at the camp and you can earn some money for your clothes—you sure do need some clothes."

I lost no time walking up to the camp, about six miles from home. That winter was

spent working as a chore boy. There were about thirty men working at this camp. I had to keep the men's shack clean, carry in wood and water, clean the barn where the horses were kept, and also helped the cook by setting and waiting on tables and washing the dishes. When the camp broke up that spring, I received a check for $120. Until then I didn't know the amount of my pay. It was one dollar per day plus board. I went home and gave the whole stake to my father. He cashed the check and gave me some of the money to buy some new clothes. I got a ride to Iron Mountain in my stepbrother's new Ford. We went to Solberg's Tailor Shop where my Uncle Werner worked as a tailor. He fitted me out with a new suit and then took me to a store for shoes and a cap. I went home feeling like a millionaire, for up to this time I had been wearing cast-off clothing.

In the fall of 1924, I went back to school. It was a small high school, and the ninth grade was taught by Miss Olga Johnson. She was very proficient in Latin. She could speak it, read it, and write it, as well as English. She would drive to school in a Model-T roadster. During the cold, winter months, she would ask me to warm the car up for her. It had to be cranked and it was rather difficult to get started. Only one boy besides myself attended high school. It was unusual at that time in that area for boys to go to school beyond the eighth grade. It was deemed necessary for boys to go to work to relieve the poverty of their families.

By the time I finished the ninth grade, my clothes were in a deplorable condition. I was wearing clothes that had belonged to another uncle of mine. He had been killed in an auto accident, and his clothes were passed on to me. The fact that they were much too big made no difference. That's all I had to wear. I also was chumming around with boys who were working and had money to spend. I had none. This bothered me, so I decided to go to work again.

This is the sawmill at Sagola, Michigan, where I worked in the winter of 1927. This is a copy of a 1911 picture.

This is a picture of the Boarding House for the employees of the sawmill at Sagola, Michigan. It was taken in the 1920s. I worked there in 1927.

This is the boarding house I slept in while working at the sawmill in 1927. I'm the boy with his head in the window. Some of my roommates are sitting on the roof of the porch.

There was an opening on the railroad for a section hand. I got that job. It paid four dollars per day. That was big money to me. My stepmother seemed pleased that I would now be able to pay for my board. It occurs to me now that I never noticed my stepbrother paying for his board. I suspect that he was allowed to save all his money for a new car. He bought a new Model-T and paid for it in cash.

Working as a section hand on the railroad was hard work. We had to lift steel rails and heavy hardwood ties. Spikes had to be driven into these ties with a heavy sledgehammer. Tracks had to be lined up with jacks and crowbars. I was glad to be able to earn the money, however.

A dance was held each Saturday night somewhere in the area. I hung around but was too bashful to try to dance. Then one night someone gave me a couple drinks of moonshine. It made me feel hilarious; it gave me courage; I asked a girl for a dance. I enjoyed the night immensely. A trip to get some more moonshine became a Saturday night ritual thereafter.

My work on the section ended with the arrival of the fall season. I soon found another job as a chore boy at Ryan's Camp. Walter Rodomski was the cook for this outfit. Besides being a very good cook, he was a cheerful man who loved to play his cornet. He would use his horn to call the men at mealtime. When the men worked too far away from camp to come in at noon, I would haul the food out to them in an old Model-T. Riding that car over the rough logging roads was like riding on the back of a bullfrog. When the teamsters came in at night, I had to pump water for their thirsty horses. They would suck it up as fast as I could pump it up. The well was very deep, and it was hard to pump. Sometimes I grew so tired from pumping I felt that I might faint.

With the coming of spring, the camp broke up and once again I went home with a stake of about $120.

A stone quarry had begun operations near the village, and I went there for a job. It was a white granite type of rock, and when crushed it was used for stucco and also made into various kinds of powder, like talcum and face powders. My father worked at this quarry as a driller and dynamiter. He would drill holes into the cliff, fill them with dynamite and blast down big chunks of rock. Our job was to break down the big rocks into smaller pieces with a twelve-pound sledge. The rocks were then loaded into a car on a narrow gauge track and hoisted up to a crusher. The dust in this crusher was so thick it was hard to see for more than two feet. In those days, men were not required to wear protective masks. The result was that we had difficulty in breathing when our nostrils became caked with dust from crushing stone. I didn't feel any ill effects from this job at that time. However, forty years later I got a jolting surprise. I had been to the sanatorium at Whitelaw, Wisconsin, for a routine TB test required for my job. I was notified a week later to come back for another check. Anxiety crept over me.

"Have you ever worked in a very dusty place or a foundry of some kind?" the nurse asked me.

"Yes," I answered, "I spent some months working in a stone quarry crushing rocks when I was a very young man."

"That's what must have caused it," she said. "You have silicon spots in your lungs. We'll place you on our outpatient treatment for one year."

Several checkups followed, and I was finally released, but I was advised to have an annual checkup thereafter.

It was 1927 and the Stone Quarry had closed for the winter. The holidays had passed. The days were cold, and the village was desolate. Some of my friends had gone away to find jobs in a sawmill at Sagola, Michigan, about thirty miles from Felch. I decided to strike out for Sagola. The hiring boss at the mill assigned me to a cleanup job on the night shift. I got a room at the company boarding house, which I shared with three other boys. Two of the boys worked on the day shift, so they slept in this room at night. The other boy and I

worked nights so we used the same bed during the day.

The mill was running twenty-four hours a day and employed about fifty men. This large crew made the condition at the boarding house very crowded. The bed linen and woolen blankets were never changed, and the place became a nightmare with bedbugs and lice. Rats were a common sight, feeding around the piles of garbage at the outdoor privies. A perpetual poker game was going on in a dirty lounge. The characters playing poker looked like aimless, hopeless, homeless men. I would fall asleep in my chair, watching them play, avoiding my lousy bed as much as possible.

When spring arrived, the hauling of logs slowed down, and the mill began to lay off workers. We were notified that the night shift would be discontinued. Once again I was faced with a dilemma. Where should I go now? Lawrence Bishop, a friend of mine, gave me the answer. He said, "I know a boy who went to Two Rivers, Wisconsin. He writes to me and tells me that jobs are easy to find down there."

"Let's go down there and look things over," I answered, with a ring of hope in my voice.

"Sure, and we'll take Fillback along with us," Bishop said.

Fillback was another roommate of ours.

We got together and decided we ought to get cleaned up and deloused before we left Sagola. We did some shopping for some new clothes at the company store. Then we went to the clubhouse showers. It was the first bath for any of us since we had been swimming the previous summer. We put on our new clothing and tied up our old ones in a bundle. Not knowing where to discard our old clothes, we carried them outside and placed them on the porch. Then we went back into the clubhouse for some ice cream. When we came out, a pair of dogs were having a tug of war in the street with our old clothes. That solved our problem. Literally, we gave our clothes to the dogs.

We boarded a train at Sagola which took us to Green Bay, Wisconsin. After a long wait at the depot, another train came and we rode it to Manitowoc. At Manitowoc, we got a ride on a streetcar to Two Rivers.

We located our friend at Two Rivers and arranged for room and board at the same place. It was Sunday, the middle of March, 1927, and I had reached my nineteenth birthday.

Monday morning we began to search for some work. We trudged to all the local industries but found the answers negative.

"We are not hiring today," the employment managers would tell us. We made the rounds daily for five weeks without any success. By this time construction work was opening up. The Streu Construction Company was paving Forest Avenue. The Municipal Hospital was being built. The Washington Street Bridge was under construction. We were standing by watching the progress on the bridge one day when the foreman looked at me and said, "Hey, you, big boy, do you want to go to work? I have a job for you, but I can't use the other two because they look too young for this work."

The next day I went to work at the bottom of the coffer dam digging out the dirt to make way for the foundation of the bridge. My two friends, Bishop and Fillback, became very discouraged and decided to go back home. A man who lived at our boarding house had a car. He said he would take them as far as Green Bay. Having no money they decided to hitch a ride on a freight train going north. After dark, their opportunity came along; and they climbed into an open box car. They made it home.

Thereafter my life began to change. I had a job, and I was no longer a derelict. I soon found a girlfriend who loved me, and I loved her, but that will have to be a different story.

My mother and a brother are buried at Iron River, Michigan. On Memorial Day, some years ago, we decided to visit the grave site. Since we had traveled the main route many times, we changed our plan of direction by taking a new route. Changes in the scenery soon began taking place. We discovered some small picturesque lakes for which the north country is noted. A deep sense of nostalgia crept over me like tingling wine. It seemed as if I could smell the logs as we drove by a logging operation. Summer was approaching and the logs were being hauled by trucks. I remembered the days that I had spent in the lumber woods, when logs could only be hauled in the winter time on logging sleds drawn by heavy horses.

As we drove into Stambaugh, Michigan, we passed the school where I had attended kindergarten. The old red building beckoned to me, but my wife didn't seem to notice it. It was recess time and I could hear the shouts and laughter of the kids. It took me back more than sixty years. Seeing the new buildings near the old one brought me back to reality. I had been away for a long time, cutting my wisdom teeth and turning gray.

We drove into Iron River, Michigan, which is situated below Stambaugh Hill. The city seemed very strange to me. Since I didn't know where to find the cemetery, I inquired at a filling station.

"Which one are you looking for," the attendant asked. "The old one or the new one?"

"It must be the old one," I answered. "My mother died here in 1914." We were not far from it, and after following his simple directions we soon located the place. After searching the area, we came upon my mother's grave. I was surprised to find it had not been neglected. The grass had been cut and a rosebush grew near the monument. It stood a silent symbol of devotion. The years had caused the ground around the stone to settle and it leaned forward as if it were begging for a lift. I found some small rocks and by pushing the stone backwards, I tucked the rocks underneath. That made it level again. As I stood by mother's grave, I thought what a proud grandmother she would be today! She would be telling everyone about her seven grandchildren, their schooling and their successful careers, and the great grandchildren who followed. Then I know for certain she would not forget to tell you how good the Lord has been to her family.

I said to myself, "Mother, yours was a short and hard life, but you did not die in vain."

Symposium on the Life Story

BY EDWARD D. IVES, ROGER E. MITCHELL,
JANE C. BECK, BARRY LEE PEARSON,
JEFF TODD TITON, JUHA YRJÄNÄ PENTIKÄINEN,
AND YVONNE HIIPAKKA LOCKWOOD

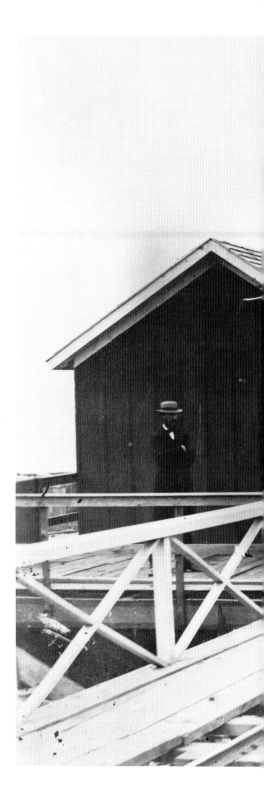

Introduction

An old and battered copy of Baron de Jomini's *Summary of the Art of War*. It had once belonged to one Edwin S. Babcock, and I had picked it up for a dime, not for any particular interest I had in Jomini— or in Babcock either, whose name meant nothing to me—but for what I had found penned on the flyleaf under Babcock's military pedigree:

I was in the column which crossed the Long Bridge from Washington to Virginia in the spring of 1861, and threw up Fort Runyon at the junction of the Orange & Alexandria Roads—and also in the column of Weitzels Division, 25th Army Corps which entered Richmond on the morning of April 3rd 1865 & bivouacked at Confederate Battery No 9 of the Defences of Richmond.

Long Bridge, Washington, D.C., the 1860s (B8184-B-266). Prints and Photographs Division, Library of Congress

The hand that wrote that note was older than the one that had neatly and proudly laid out his rise from private to acting field officer; the writing is crabbed and the words crowded, almost running off the page at the end. In my mind's eye, I saw an old man considering that youthful and abstract pedigree and wanting to leave something more, something that said "I was there. . . . I ate the dust of that road," like wonderful old Bernal Diaz del Castillo's "That which I have myself seen and the fighting." Who was Babcock writing for, I wondered, that I should come upon him amongst an odd lot in an outdoor bookstall a century later? That was beyond all conjecture, but I doubt that it mattered much compared to his need simply to get something down against the approach of what Sir Thomas Browne called "the iniquity of oblivion." "I was in the column. . . ." For Babcock, evidently that was enough, but, whether it was or not, that was all there was.

However, it has not always been enough, and consequently autobiography is a well-established literary genre—an account either of one's entire life or of a significant part of it. Traditionally autobiographies are written by the illustrious or demi-illustrious—it is almost a responsibility for statesmen to write their "memoirs"—toward the end of long and busy lives, and their overt motives have been many: to set the record straight, to justify their ways to men, to make money for themselves or their posterity, etc. Always, of course, they are backward looks, and inevitably that means, as both Jeff Titon and Barry Pearson point out in their commentaries, fictions, things made to show how the authors see themselves or wish others to see them. In no sense does that mean that such documents are not "true"; it means that no one can either "tell it all" or "tell it like it was," simply because there is far too much to tell. One must select, presenting as coherent and sequential what was at best inchoate and confusing. No account of the past will be as complex and multiple as that past was when it was present, and therefore—whatever motives one may have or claim for writing it—autobiography, hammered out as it usually is late in the game under the

shadow of that approaching iniquity, is one more expression of what Wallace Stevens called our "blessed rage for order," and a very touching one it is.

Given wellsprings as deep and powerful as all that, it is not surprising to find the autobiographical impulse very much alive on all levels of society and in all walks of life. Always and everywhere there are those who—for any number of complex reasons—look on life as something not only to be lived but also to be told about, not only as experience but also as the raw materials for their art. For most such people the oral tradition—"yarning"—is the only medium in which they work; the best develop local reputations as great storytellers, the worst are known as bores. But occasionally there are those—and they are not always the yarners either—who seek a larger canvas. They want to show more than the oral anecdote can offer: sequence, connectedness, even causality. These are the ones who turn to the written word, who decide to "write a book"; they sit down at the kitchen table, pencil in hand, and in the course of a week or a month or a year they grind out a small—though sometimes not so small—pile of manuscript. Once in a while such a manuscript gets published, or a friend or relative will type it over for handing around the family or the neighborhood; but most likely the manuscript is put in an envelope marked "Grampy's 'book' " and put away somewhere, because while no one really wants to throw it away, no one quite knows what the next step should be. And there it sits until, as fortune may fall, something like a junketing folklorist happens upon it.

Here in Maine, that is how it was for Fleetwood Pride. Convinced he had lived an adventurous life as a woodsman, he sat down at age ninety to write about it. "I have worked shoulder to shoulder with men who were men," he said. "They smoked pipes and wore braces and didn't spend half their time lighting cigarettes and hitching up their pants."[1] Five years later, when I was up visiting him for the first time, his wife handed me a big envelope full of manuscript, wondering what the chances were of getting it published. And that was also how it was for Wilbur Day, hunter, guide, and poacher, who wanted to make it clear to the world that he was not the "great big spill blood desperardo represented by some" and therefore dictated his story to his wife just before he died. Then for forty years the manuscript sat in John and Alice Bacon's shed, stuffed into an old wooden ammunition box, until one of my students happened upon it.[2] And that is almost how it was for Arvid Asplund, except that he took matters more into his own hands.

Mr. Asplund says that he originally thought of "Via Dolorosa" as a story for his children to read, but he admitted to Roger Mitchell that always in the back of his mind he had known "I got a story to tell." After he retired he got busy on it, seeking help from his local senior center to begin with and then taking that mysterious "next step" himself by following up a notice he had seen about *Folklife Annual*. Library of Congress archivist Gerry Parsons suggested the format to editor Jim Hardin —that of text with commentaries. Mr. Asplund found that agreeable, and here we are.

The commentaries cover a number of important matters and can offer the reader some good examples of the range of interests folklorists can have in a document like "Via Dolorosa." Roger Mitchell gives us an account of his visit with Mr. Asplund, which he undertook to explore the author's rea-

sons for concentrating so exclusively on the hardships of his early years, and that leads him into a discussion of the differences between biography and autobiography as approaches to a life. Jeff Titon touches on this same subject, emphasizing how the work is both a historical document (i.e. "true") and a fiction, and then he goes on to show the importance of stepmother and separation imagery to the narrative. Both he and Jane Beck discuss the increasing interest folklorists are showing in individual life histories, and then Beck points up the special value of the written as opposed to the oral life history. Yvonne Lockwood and Juha Pentikäinen emphasize the ethnic dimensions of the narrative, while Barry Pearson brings us back for further looks at the author's shaping spirit, which selects and arranges while "telling the truth." All six pay Mr. Asplund the compliment of taking his serious effort very seriously indeed, respecting it for what it is without subjecting it, say, to some precious and irrelevant standard of literary excellence. In this they show themselves good folklorists.

If our scholars come through as good craftsmen, Arvid Asplund comes through as a good human being, one of E. M. Forster's aristocracy of the decent and plucky. Against the dark of that always coming on iniquity, his "Via Dolorosa" glows as a candle, and such small affirming flames as his—and the even smaller one of that old soldier Edwin Babcock—can light our way by letting us know we go in good company.

EDWARD D. IVES
University of Maine at Orono

NOTES

1. Edward D. Ives and David C. Smith, eds., *Fleetwood Pride 1864–1960: The Autobiography of a Maine Woodsman. Northeast Folklore* 9 (Orono, Maine: 1967), 16.

2. Wilbur Day's "Autobiography" will be published soon as volume 26 of *Northeast Folklore*.

Despite All That

"I always had in the back of my mind: I got a story to tell. After I retired, I had time to tell it."

Thus, with words as lean and fit as his frame, Arvid Asplund responded to my query as to what inspired him to retrace his youth in "Via Dolorosa." Yet as the morning wore on, it became apparent that there was much more he could have told. His well-kept house, yard, and car ("Do my own work."), his quiet pride in his children's success, his graciousness as a host, his poise during a long interview, all evidenced a man who was at ease with his several competencies.

He has worn many hats throughout a long life at work. In addition to the tasks described in "Via Dolorosa," Asplund labored thirteen years in a furniture factory. ("We worked a fifty-hour week. Five nine-hour days and five hours on Saturday. It seemed like heaven to have Saturday afternoons off.") Came World War II and he moved to a defense-related job in a machine shop. ("I had four kids and a perforated eardrum. The Army just didn't want me.") After the war, he sold insurance for awhile and drove a school bus. But his wife didn't like all the evening hours. He then tried his hand as a shipping clerk for Mirro Aluminum Company. ("I didn't like that.") His last job was working in a hardware store. ("That included two nights a week, and I was able to work my hours so as to keep driving the school bus.") He continued this double routine until 1972, when much to his surprise, he had a heart attack. ("It was then I realized I was getting too old to work two jobs. So I slowed down and my heart hasn't bothered me since.")

He dropped the bus route and retired a year later (1973) from the hardware store. But not completely. He still works one day a week at the store and fills in when someone is sick or on vacation. His comment: "It makes it nice for everyone."

But these several jobs which took up the greater part of Asplund's working life did not appear to weigh heavily on his mind. He did them successfully, brought up his family, and prepared for old age. The Depression he also disposed of with a few words: "I did anything I could. I had four kids and a wife to support, but we made it."

During the time spent in a creative writing class, Asplund prepared as assignments written histories of Two Rivers, Wisconsin, and his local church, along with an account of what it was like to be a family man during the Depression years. In our long interview, Asplund and I matched stories of lumbering in Maine (my home state) and in Michigan. We shared many points of similarity, and Asplund came through as a man who knows the art of old-fashioned lumbering well. But both in person and in his autobiography, he does not appear to be a man to dwell on the mechanics of hard work and hard times. What it boils down to is, that which could be solved with hard work and careful planning, he had always been able to do.

Nor does Arvid Asplund appear much drawn by ties of ethnicity. When we discussed the Swedish background of his Finnish ancestors, he observed that there was a fairly large Swedish-speaking minority in Finland, but gave little indication that he saw this as having any particular significance. ("Father said it was because of some war a long time ago. It was before his time.") So much for Gustavus Adolphus, the Lion of the North, centuries of Swedish dominance, and the counter-currents of Finnish nationalism. Like many contemporary families of immigrant backgrounds, the Asplunds have recently gotten in touch with relatives in both Finland and Sweden, and a daughter and granddaughter are planning a trip to Europe to visit relatives this summer (1985). But Arvid's recounting of all this was restrained. Ethnicity was a starting point and influenced his early years, but he has outgrown it.

A major reason for my arranging an interview with Mr. Asplund was to see if I could gain some perspective as to why he had devoted so much attention to the early portion of his life and so little to the latter. Once he had met and married the present

Mrs. Asplund, things became, according to "Via Dolorosa," another story.

Asplund's choice of title tells it all. It was indeed a hard beginning and, saddest of all, there was precious little he could do during his early years to escape. But once he had started a family of his own, he and his wife could, through devotion, hard work, and planning, mold events much more to their liking. When Arvid stopped to look over memory's shoulder, it was that early portion of his life that violated his concept of how things should be, and his telling of it became an expiation of sorts. He could say to his posterity, "I didn't have the best of starts, but I made it."

This brings us to the value of the life history, or the folk autobiography, if you will. Unlike such disciplines as sociology, with its highly quantitative approach, we who work with folklore-folklife materials are vulnerable to prejudicing our data along the lines of whatever took us into the field in the first place. If ethnicity is our focus, in our interviewing of the Arvid Asplunds we concentrate on this topic; and then writing up the results, we may well make more of our modest ethnic data than Arvid would himself.

In addition to imposing our own focus on our subjects' memories of things past, we doubtless make a longer and more nearly complete story of it all. With our academic training, we want a beginning, a rising action, a resolution, an end; and with enough interviews, we can make it come out that way. But we can very easily in our craftsmanship overshadow the basic chapter that may well have made the man.

When a visiting Israeli sociologist, disturbed by the waning of the work ethic in Israel, began to probe my father about his attitudes concerning self-sufficiency, he was somewhat upset that Father did not come through with a ringing statement about a fair day's work for a fair day's pay. "But you made your position very clear in *I'm a Man that Works*," he protested. (Roger E. Mitchell, *"I'm a Man that Works": The Biography of Don Mitchell of Merrill, Maine, Northeast Folklore* 19, 1978.)

Father's response was, "Sure, I said those things at one time or another. But the boy put them together. If it'd been left up to me, it never would have got put together. I'm no good at that sort of thing."

Had he put it together, he doubtless would have left out many parts that I as his son felt were necessary to the full story. And he probably would have built up others that would have emphasized things about him that I missed.

Here we have the basic difference between biography and autobiography. My biography of my father has a lot of me in it. But Arvid Asplund poured out himself in "Via Dolorosa," and, in so doing, reveals another facet of the hard story of immigration. So very often the immigrant found only more hard work in the land of opportunity, but he could at least hope that his children would do better. However, Asplund's father was in a doubly difficult position. His wife had been long sick, and in her passing left him two children to rear, an impossible task for a day laborer. He turned to a traditional solution—the marriage of convenience—and got the traditional result—the unkind stepmother, one of the oldest motifs in world folklore.

As Arvid Asplund looks back from his comfortable middle-class perspective, he can say, "But despite all that, I made it." And in telling his story, he can reaffirm the old values of perseverance and hard work. As he pointed out to me, he had originally meant this story for his children and his children's children, but he didn't doubt there were some things of value there if others wanted to read it.

There are indeed.

ROGER E. MITCHELL
University of Wisconsin—Eau Claire

Within the Family

For some time now folklorists have been interested in collecting individuals' life stories.[1] These stories, told by a diverse assortment of men and women, are usually selected because the folklorist sees them as keys to understanding a particular group or community. Although each individual has unique qualities, he shares lifestyles, work and social patterns, and traditions and customs which link him to a larger group.

A life story cuts across the various genres of folklore and places such genres in a natural context. It underscores the values and attitudes that lie at the inner core of the individual and expresses the view of the narrator as he depicts those incidents that were important to him and that he holds most significant to his life.

A number of life stories within a region weave a pattern, much like a memory quilt, and produce an understanding of the area. For that reason, when interviewing for the Vermont Folklife Center's archives I look for the individual who might be representative of a particular occupation, like farming or slate quarrying, and who is willing to talk about his life in relation to his occupation. Preferably, I want a narrator who needs little prompting and is descriptive and knowledgeable in his detail. A number of such interviews help the researcher better understand the traditional culture of Vermont.

Frequently the folklorist takes a number of these tape-recorded interviews, edits them, adds chronological order, and presents the whole as an autobiography of the narrator.[2] To my mind such life stories are important to folklore scholarship, but one must be aware of their shortcomings: the influence of the interviewer and his questions, the selective editing process, and the personality of the narrator himself—how he views his own life in retrospect.

A second type of life story to which the folklorist has given little consideration in the past—largely because few of these have

been made available to him—is the written life story. These narratives are usually compiled because the author wants to leave a record for his children and grandchildren. Mostly these documents are treasured within the family, and they seldom reach a wider audience.

While interviewing extensively in Vermont, I have been made aware of a number of these documents. Almost all are written late in life, with an emphasis on what an individual has done—incidents and events he has taken part in rather than his inner thoughts and feelings. The written life story appears to be less obviously concerned with presenting a self-conscious image of the narrator than that which emerges from a series of oral interviews.[3] Perhaps this is because the writer's audience is his family who already know him well.

A typical introduction is:

Living in two worlds as I have, is a privilege few can share. The generation now growing up has no idea what life was like to live with no telephone, no electricity, no gas engines, not any radio, no television where we could watch a murder a minute. Neither was there any waxed paper, and no plastic.

In this little collection of incidents, one could hardly call them stories, I have tried to tell those that came after me what life was like when I was growing up.

I dedicate this to my great grandchildren, and all the clan.[4]

The written life story has certain obvious differences from its oral counterpart. It is solely the work of the individual who lived the life—his own unprompted reflections. Although primarily written for those closest to him, the account also serves as a graven image of his life for future generations. It consists of a collection of incidents that the individual feels are the most significant to him and to his life as a whole. Because of the medium—the written word—incidents are more clearly articulated, although frequently without the wealth of detail conversation might evoke. Perhaps of greatest interest to the folklorist is the way the narrator views his life, what he considers important and how he interprets various incidents. This meaning is derived by filtering

Daisy Turner, 102-year-old native Vermonter, whose life story has been collected by Jane Beck. Daisy Turner's father came to Grafton, Vermont, in 1872 with a number of ex-slaves to work in the lumber woods. Her family history spans two hundred years, from Africa to a farm in Vermont which is the setting for her own life story. Photograph by Jane Beck

items through traditions and attitudes shared with those people he is writing about.

"Via Dolorosa" is an excellent example of the written life story. Arvid Asplund, after retiring from work, writes of his first twenty years. With retirement comes time and the inclination to search out some of his family history and to tell the story of "long family hardships." For the folklorist the expression of the immigrant and first-generation experience is of interest—his schooling, the jobs he held, the activities he singled out, details about the food, folk cures, and folk speech. But of even greater interest is the meaning Asplund gives his own life in retrospect. Interestingly, he has little knowledge of Finland; in fact he must turn to a cookbook to give him the details he feels he needs. His father's story starts with his trip to this country, or at least this is what Asplund's memory recalls.

At the end of his life Asplund is interested in knowing more details. He had been away a long time, cutting his wisdom teeth and turning gray. Now he can put his first years into some perspective. What remains with him are those years of emotional and physical hardship. Asplund's parents came to this land of promise only to face a life of continual trial and endurance. His mother succumbed at the age of twenty-eight while his father encouraged his son with "better days are coming." The first two decades of young Asplund's life did not seem to give much credence to this hope and consisted of hard work, loneliness, poverty, and hostility at home. Despite the hardships of his early life and those of his parents, by his retirement Asplund can reaffirm the importance of his long-dead mother and the successes of her grandchildren. His mother did not live in vain. Despite the painful beginning, the family has triumphed. They can take their place as Americans, hold their heads high, and acknowledge their debt to those forebears who made this possible.

By writing this account of his first twenty years, Asplund has dealt with what it meant to be the son of Finnish immigrants. He has given us an insider's view of his way of life, and in his last years he has come to terms with that life, giving it meaning for himself and future generations through the perceptions of his own folk culture.

JANE C. BECK
Vermont Council on the Arts

NOTES

1. Life story is defined by Jeff Titon in "The Life Story," *Journal of American Folklore* 93(1980):276, as "a person's story of his or her life, or what he or she thinks is a significant part of that life. . . . a personal narrative . . ." Titon is interested in its value as "a fiction" in distinction to its value as a historical document.

2. Some examples are Jeff Titon, *From Blues to Pop: The Autobiography of Leonard "Baby Doo" Caston*, JEMF Special Series, no. 4 (Los Angeles: John B. Edwards Memorial Foundation, 1974); Bruce Jackson, *A Thief's Primer* (New York: Macmillan, 1969); Alan Lomax, *Mister Jelly Roll* (New York: Grossett and Dunlap, 1950); M. G. Smith, *Dark Puritan* (Jamaica: University of the West Indies, 1963);

Wayne Reuel Bean, ed., *Me and Fannie*, Northeast Folklore 14 (1973); Julia A. Hunter, ed., *Anna May: Eighty-two Years in New England*, Northeast Folklore 20 (1979); Jane C. Beck, *To Windward of the Land* (Bloomington, Ind.: Indiana University Press, 1979).

3. During the interviews I conducted with Alexander Charles, a West Indian fisherman, he presented the image of himself as hero to me. Often he would say to me, "If I wasn't a hero, I don't believe you would see me today." See Jane Beck, *To Windward of the Land*, p. 268.

4. Bernice Douglas Reed, "The Old Birchard Place" (manuscript typed for children and grandchildren's Christmas present, 1973).

Through Selective Memory

Although most people do not write such lengthy manuscripts, autobiographical statements of some form, written or spoken, longer or shorter, are fairly common. People tell their story to set the record straight, to confess, to promote a cause, or to fulfill a sense of obligation to detail their family history. If they happen to be celebrities or public figures they are likely to be asked about themselves, and so they construct a version of their past which responds in part to common questions they encounter regarding their motivations, their influences, and the products for which they may be known.

For example, my own work has been with blues musicians who not only maintain a public profile but are also typecast in relation to popular beliefs about their art form and their lifestyle. Since they are constantly being asked about their lives, most have put together cohesive and entertaining stories detailing their musical adventures. Since their stories develop in part as a response to interviews, the stories come in spoken form. Moreover, the common questions enable the bluesman to develop a predictive awareness of what parts of his life—or rather his story—seem to turn people on. And since he tells his story to an audience of sorts, the audience's immediate responses provide further guidelines for what works, what entertains, or what confuses the listener.

Mr. Asplund claims he wrote his account to tell his story, the story of his family's hardships and the story of Finnish immigrants. From this perspective his autobiography embraces self, family, and regional ethnic group. However, it remains essentially introspective, a personal account written later in life when leisure and spare time allowed it.

Unlike the blues musician who tells his tale to an interviewer, Mr. Asplund wrote his autobiography on his own initiative, and it appears to be the result of personal motives and private musing. His saga bows to the conventions of the written word, but because he is a relatively untrained writer, it would probably be labeled "naive autobiography" by literary scholars.

Like so many autobiographical documents, it focuses on how he became what he is and then stops. In fact we could retitle it "The Early Years of Struggle," because it essentially ends when his life took a turn for the better. We assume there was more to his life, but perhaps his later experiences did not tie in with the overall theme of hardship. Or perhaps he thought they would not make good reading, or maybe he simply got tired of writing. In any event he chose what to include, what to delete, where to start, where to stop.

In contrast to his father's immigrant lore, which includes such common motifs as the image of America as the land of milk and honey, the help of fellow countrymen who have gone on ahead, details of the crossing and of rejoining the ethnic community—which project a sense of optimism even in the face of failure—the author's story presents a pessimistic view of immigrant life, where only the strong and the lucky survive. He gives us a story of personal struggle and endurance organized as a series of work experiences. From the mine, to the timber, to the farm, to the quarry, we see the round of life and work in terms of life's trials: cruelty, exhaustion, dirt, vermin, disease, and death. Although there are positive images—children's games and pastimes, drink, dancing, courtship, marriage, and education—the emphasis falls on the hard life.

This, of course, reflects the author's experience as well as his philosophy of life or his view of what his experiences mean. But it also reflects his interpretation of what makes for a good story. Looking back he reorders the past, bringing it into congruence with his present self-image, his purpose in writing the document, his narrative persona, and the extent of his ability to manipulate the tone and style of the document. What we see is the end result, experience translated through selective memory onto the printed page, reworked, revised, and edited into a coherent, workable text.

Although the author stresses the work's historical dimension—"it is," he writes, "truth not fiction"—historians may be uneasy with his methods. For example, he uses a cookbook for his primary source concerning Finland. More to the point, he uses his memory, or on occasion his memory of his father's memories of the past, to reconstruct his story. To supplement what he remembers, he introduces several documents, along with other devices—site visits, conversations, and artifacts—to help him call up the past. Yet even in these cases we are unsure if these props triggered his memory or are better understood as literary devices generating flashbacks or otherwise holding the narrative together.

Folklorists have become increasingly aware of the value of autobiographical documents whether written or spoken. Over the years their methods and goals have gradually changed to reflect a broader shift in interest from folklore items to the people and communities who maintain various traditions. In the past folklorists essentially mined autobiography for references to recognized traditions such as songs, tales, customs, beliefs, or occupational techniques. Or, if the writer or speaker was a traditional artist, they tied autobiographical detail to items in the artist's repertoire, providing a context of sorts for the materials they perform. Today folklorists are more apt to accept autobiography as a type of traditional document in its own right. Nevertheless we still encounter a wide range of approaches to the subject, depending on the folklorist's specific interest. My work focused on the life story as a form of oral narrative. I found that blues artists drew heavily on tradition when they put together their stories, and as a result one musician's story shared much in common with that of another. While bluesmen present us with a special case—after all, they are professional entertainers, storytellers in song, and both victims and beneficiaries of a highly developed stereotype—their stories, like Mr. Asplund's, illustrate a common need to order and communicate the experiences which then represent an individual's life. Obviously countless choices have to be made, and I am intrigued by why people consider certain experiences or events noteworthy and how they interpret the events they witnessed or the forces which acted on their lives. Mr. Asplund's overview of his life as a sad road reminds me of the blues verse "I ain't going down that dark road by myself." His story engages us and future readers in his life, at least along those roads where he cares to take us.

BARRY LEE PEARSON
University of Maryland

Virginia Bluesman John Cephas performing at the Smithsonian's Festival of American Folklife in 1985. Barry Pearson is currently working on a study of the life and art of John Cephas and Archie Edwards. Photograph copyright © Lisa Falk 1985

Of Separation and Survival

In the past twenty years or so, many American folklorists have become more interested in people's stories of their own lives and less interested in people's stories of ghosts, fairies, talking animals, and the like—the body of material that traditionally has been thought of as folk narrative. There was a time when folklorists felt the need to justify studying the purportedly true, personal experience story, but no longer. Now folklorists seek out such stories for their value as history and as personal history, and sometimes for their value as literature. Interested in what life is (and was) like for folk groups that share traditions, folklorists regard the reminiscences of members of those groups as useful historical documents.

I am writing this, on invitation from the editors of *Folklife Annual,* not so much as an interpretation of Mr. Asplund's narrative, although I will offer one, but on the role life history plays in the work of the folklorist. In "The Life Story" (*Journal of American Folklore* 93 (1980):276–92), I suggested that we as folklorists have been a bit cavalier in taking a person's stories and information given in interviews and then editing them into a coherent, continuous, chronological, first-person narrative, as if the person had shaped it that way himself. To take an example from my own work: interviewing a minister several times about his life, I ranged back and forth over various periods in it as the conversation flowed. Putting what he said together later, in a chronological fashion, I was surprised to see that a statement about how as a boy he detested working on his parents' farm fit just before he had a vision in which God called him to preach. Now it may very well be that these two events are connected logically as well as chronologically; but to edit them to follow one upon the other in a first-person narrative is to give the illusion that the minister connected them that way himself at the time. He may well have revealed himself, but he did not do so artfully.

However, Mr. Asplund's story comes to us, so far as we know, as an unadulterated literary autobiography. He may have had some help writing it, but in the absence of evidence to the contrary I will assume that the story is, finally, Mr. Asplund's. The narrative is continuous, coherent, chronological, and of Mr. Asplund's making. As a folklorist I am interested in it both as a historical account and as a "fiction" or making that reveals how Mr. Asplund sees himself. The autobiography offers a personal history of a boy and young man who belonged to a folk group of immigrant Finnish families in Michigan and who was caught up in the traditions of such occupational groups as miners, lumberjacks, railroad workers, and stone quarry workers. He sets the scenes of the lumber company towns in northern Michigan, and he writes also of children's traditions as he recalls his boyhood hijinks with his friend John Trewartha. Finally, he presents a great many of his family's traditions, including the Swedish traditions of his stepmother, like blood bread. This is useful and interesting historical documentation that helps the folklorist understand some of the folk traditions of that time and place.

I am interested in Mr. Asplund's piece as a personal document as well. Like all life stories, it is a fiction, a making; and I am interested in its shape: what it contains, what is emphasized, what is omitted, why it is put together as it is, what the impulse was for writing it, and what it tells us about the author and, ultimately, about ourselves. The theme—that is, what Mr. Asplund wants us to come away with from reading it—is contained in his title, "Via Dolorosa." He emphasizes the hardships of his early life. Actually, of course, it is a story of survival: something bad happens, but Mr. Asplund survives. Then some other misfortune occurs, but Mr. Asplund remains himself. Usually the hardships involve poverty and onerous work, but sometimes they comprise unjust punishments, usually meted out by his stepmother. He portrays her as a mean woman, constantly tormenting and harassing him, calling him a "tubercular bum," giving him endless chores, and preventing him from engaging in his favorite pas-

Brother John Sherfey preaching in his radio ministry at the WRAA studios, Luray, Virginia, July 1977. Mr. Sherfey's oral autobiography may be heard on the record album Powerhouse for God *(University of North Carolina Press, 1982). The oral autobiography and several hours of interviews with his wife, Pauline, and members of his family are on deposit at the Library of Congress's Archive of Folk Culture. Photograph by Jeff Titon*

time—reading. But the portrayal is more than that: Mr. Asplund casts his stepmother as a devil. Early on, he introduces her and follows that with the account of his puppy's mysterious drowning, placing suspicion on the stepmother. The very next scene concerns his stepmother's cooking "blood bread." He presents it in a perfectly plausible way, as a Swedish foodways tradition; yet, coming where it does, after the death of the puppy, and with its name, it carries overtones of witchcraft and bloody sacrifice. When she orders his sister to burn their mother's Bible the portrait of this stepmother-as-devil is complete.

Wicked stepmothers are, of course, a stock ingredient in what we think of as the corpus of European folktales; as a folklorist, I am not surprised to find that Mr. Asplund has, wittingly or not, used this tradition for his literary art. More interesting, though, is how he uses it. He ends his story at his mother's grave, saying, "Mother, you did not die in vain." Mr. Asplund's natural mother, portrayed as an innocent saint—she must have taught him the "little Swedish prayer"; it couldn't have been his stepmother who did so—suffers and dies; and the child must endure the torments of his stepmother, but he survives them.

Separation, then, becomes the most poignant theme of this autobiography. The point is underscored in Mr. Asplund's reminiscence about being abandoned at the carnival. The family's young hired girl and her boyfriend have to take him along to the carnival, but he is "in their way" and, after giving him some tickets and telling him to ride the merry-go-round, they disappear. Vividly, Mr. Asplund paints the terrifying scene:

It was dark. I didn't know the way back home. I was being pushed around by crowds of people. The strange faces and the excitement around the carnival filled me with horror. I began to cry, and I cried and cried.

Tellingly, this is the only time that Mr. Asplund allows himself tears, and they are over separation and loss. It is an effective scene, and it reaches out to everyone who has experienced something similar. I suspect that most of us have. But for Mr. Asplund, separation and the loss of his mother appear as the narrative's shaping forces and give it much of its human interest. Folklorists are interested in families as folk groups; the family, it may be suggested, is the primary folk group, socializing the child from the very outset into its shared traditions. Folklore and personal history meet on this ground; Mr. Asplund's narrative shows us precisely how and even suggests why.

JEFF TODD TITON
Tufts University

In the Promised Land

Ein Menschenleben, ach, es ist so wenig.
Ein Menschenschicksal, ach, es ist so viel.

Grillparzer

Autobiography is one of the oldest genres in literature. There were many autobiographical writers in antiquity, and the ancient sources of most book religions contain biographical data. There is autobiographical literature both in prose and verse, and the genre seems to have grown rapidly. Religious and political leaders, writers and other artists, scientists, emigrants and immigrants, representatives of minorities, common people—all want to recall and write down what they have experienced in the world. I don't know if this desire could be considered a drive to produce an autobiography, but it is a very natural drive. As Miguel de Unamuno has said: "Man is not born with a soul; he dies with one he has manufactured. And the purpose of life is that he should manufacture a soul, and that soul immortal and his very own work. For, in the hour of death, a man leaves a skeleton to the earth and a soul—a product— to history. . . . The life of the soul—spiritual life—is a struggle against eternal oblivion."

According to one brief definition, "an autobiography is a narrative of the past of a person by the person concerned." According to Bates, this expression is "quite satisfactory as a definition, provided one has no need to apply it; but only so." In comparison to biography, which usually has been written by someone other than the person concerned, autobiography normally begins several years later than biography, and, of course, ends earlier, too. An autobiography is a verbally transmitted or written account of one's own life. At the same time it is not only a life description or a life experience but a personal retrospective picture of an individual's image of the way he saw or rather wanted to see it. According to Bates, there is no decisive distinction between autobiography and fiction: "All autobiography contains a percentage of fiction; and the fiction best worth attention tends to be autobiographical."

"Via Dolorosa" by Arvid Asplund belongs to the genre of written autobiographies. As such, it is his own unique story consisting of oral traditions transmitted in family and immigrant society in the way he recalled them as well as his personal reminiscences from his youth. An autobiography is always the result of a personal choice. Recalling and writing it down requires a long-lasting effort and is both a communicative and a creative process. "Via Dolorosa" can be regarded as a literary work, written by a layman writer about his unique life experience. At the same time, it is an expression of immigrant folklore and a description of immigrant history. When individual pieces like this are put together and compared with each other, scholars of immigrant culture may have better opportunities for drawing conclusions on the shared immigrant experiences than if they rely only on statistics of immigration and other hard documents.

Surprisingly enough, there has been much less interest so far in life-history materials in folkloric circles than in psychology, anthropology, and history, for example. When I started my career in folklore as a research assistant in the Folklore Archives of the Finnish Literature Society—which probably are the biggest in the world as far as the number of folklore items is concerned—I learned to know a signum *F*, inherited from the period of Kaarle Krohn, the famous founder of the Finnish geographic-historical method. It contained ethno- and life-historical data and other "fabulated" materials and booklore, which could not be considered to belong to the traditional generic categories of the pure "Folklore." When folklore is considered to be an anthropological discipline, it should be as, or even more, interested in "folk" than in "lore." For that reason, it is a very good time to find some keys to open the door to the mysterious *F* of folklorists.

Life history is an individual's view of the course of his own life and its central events from childhood until the moment of their

being recorded. It can be written down personally (autobiography) or told orally in an interview with a researcher. Quite often a life history is the result of this kind of interaction between two people, the interviewer and the interviewee. My own experiences of the biographical method stem from ten years of field work with an illiterate White Sea Karelian informant, Mrs. Marina Takalo (1890–1970). My two books on her life history and world view, *Marina Takalon uskonto* (1971) and *Oral Repertoire and World View* (1978), are the results of a tandem work. It was not myself but Mrs. Takalo who first proposed the idea of writing her life story. At the end of a long interview in 1962 she spontaneously suggested: "I tell you everything I remember. I want you to know all about Karelian life. You tell others what I have experienced and seen in the World that they understand what the life of a stranger is like."

Marina Takalo was a refugee from Russian Karelia. All her life she carried several minority identities with strong feelings that she was a stranger, different from the others. As a Karelian she was ethnically different from most Finns; as an Old Believer her religious affiliation was different from Finnish Christianity with its Lutheran or Orthodox background. Besides this she was a citizen of Russia (or the Soviet Union) all her life, and finally she was illiterate in the almost completely literate country of Finland.

Mr. Asplund's autobiography is a good example of immigrant life histories with strong feelings of ethnicity, in this case Finnishness. Being a Finn in America meant, at least in the beginning, in such places as the Upper Peninsula, strong feelings of togetherness on the one hand, and long-lasting deprivations due to being different in language and culture on the other. I would have liked to meet Mr. Asplund to interview him about the details of his life history which he does not tell in his "Via Dolorosa." His life cycle seems to correspond to the average informant in Elli-Kaija Köngäs-Maranda's study "Finnish-American Folklore: Quantitative and Qualitative Analysis" (Ph.D. diss., Indiana University, 1963): "If a statistical profile of the average Finnish-born interviewee were to be drawn, it would look like this: He/she had migrated from Finland to the United States at the age of 20 in the year 1910. He had graduated from primary school, has supported himself and his family by manual labor and now lives as a retiree—'taking it easy,' now that he has the 'chance.'"

Mr. Asplund's literary work is not only his life story but a piece of another genre, that of family history as well. He expresses this part of the work quite clearly in his statement of introduction: "Besides the tracing of my ancestors, it is a story of long family hardships. It is a story about Finnish immigrants who came to the United States in the early 1900s." In the course of the transmission of this kind of family folklore from generation to generation, nostalgic narratives from Finland and about hardships in the new country have taken the patina of "sacred family history," so that they might be characterized even as family myths. It is important for a family keeping up the interest in its roots to remember this kind of folklore—colorful tales of how the forebears left the Old Country, journeyed from Liverpool to Ellis Island by boat, then by train to the Copper Country or the iron mines to work there and finally to the destination with a homestead or whatever more ordinary settlement in the New World, in their "Promised Land."

The title of Mr. Asplund's life story, "Via Dolorosa," refers to a Biblical passage he picked up from a sermon he once heard that appealed to him. Even when trying to be as honest as possible in the process of recalling and writing down, the author of an autobiography is dependent on the patterns above him. On the one hand, he describes something which is his unique life and his private property to the extent he is willing to open himself up; on the other he very well knows that he shares something with the rest of the American Finnish community. The problem is similar to what Elli-Kaija Köngäs-Maranda writes in her posthumous article "Väärällä puoen Atlanttia" (On the Wrong Side of the Atlantic Ocean) in 1982: "The emigrant's problem is existential. This was made clear to me by American Finns already twenty years ago by their repeating to the point of making it proverbial: 'Whoever crosses the Atlantic is always on the wrong side of the ocean.' At its richest, the life of an emigrant means possession of two cultures—'citizenship of two worlds.' At its poorest, it is timidity, a sense of inferiority, hunger on a diet of a black bread. The Old Country does not remember, the new one does not care."

I would encourage people whose life story is similar to Mr. Asplund's or who feel that theirs is different either to write their autobiography or to tell it to someone to be recorded. These stories in which people tell about themselves transmit to us both unique experiences and some of the universals of human mind and feelings.

JUHA YRJÄNÄ PENTIKÄINEN
University of Helsinki

Both Unique and Familiar

Life stories or autobiographies are the result of decision-making processes; information is recalled (or forgotten), interpreted, and finally selected, as it suits the author's purpose. Multiple voices make up history, and voices such as Arvid Asplund's contribute texture to conventional histories that often generalize the past from the perspective of movers and doers. On the other hand, the question uppermost in my mind is what the texture of Mr. Asplund's story would have been if the story had been told orally, and the broader context could also have been studied. Without that opportunity, however, I offer my thoughts on Arvid Asplund's life story, which is both unique and familiar.

Arvid Asplund's story begins with "Finnish immigrants"; this fact requires explanation. Finland is an ethnically heterogeneous country with a population consisting primarily of *Same* (Lapps), Russian and Swedish speakers, and Finnish speakers. Swedish-speaking Finns came to the United States as Russian subjects; they were called Finns, and they spoke Swedish.[1]

As the country of origin, Finland played an important role in the Americanization of the Swede Finns. They settled in the same areas as the other Finns, and they felt more at home with Finnish speakers from Finland than with Swedes from Sweden.[2] This phenomenon has also been observed among Croatian-speaking Austrians, who attend German-Austrian churches and German-American social events rather than Yugoslav-Croatian events. Although bilingual speakers existed among both the Finnish- and Swedish-speaking Finns (some also spoke Russian), language was an obstacle. Eventually, language barriers became too great and Swedish speakers began to form their own societies and churches, at first applying the term *Swede Finn* to themselves and later *Finland Swede*. They are a proud people who still distinguish themselves as Swedes from Finland.

Arvid Asplund is a second-generation Finland Swede. He grew up hearing Swedish at home and among friends of his parents. Despite his childhood environment, Asplund does not describe himself as Finland Swede (or as Swede Finn, a term which is also commonly used in the Upper Peninsula where he was raised). Even the Bicentennial, which served as an identity catalyst for many ethnic Americans, does not seem to have influenced him. He presents his story about "Finnish immigrants" without explaining the reason that his parents spoke Swedish instead of Finnish. Also of interest is his description of first learning about sauna. The entire passage differentiates him from others: his father's speech (reported in stereotypic Upper Peninsula immigrant generation's dialect) and his own remark that he would not want to sauna in the described Finnish way. To have reached his teens in the Upper Peninsula and not to have known his father's country of origin or about sauna are very curious. Rather than evaluate this information as fact, however, it would be more useful to approach it as an expression of Mr. Asplund's identity. As has been argued elsewhere,[3] life stories communicate self-perception; they may be historically false, but they are psychologically true. Arvid Asplund designates himself as different from those he describes. Similar distancing is also expressed in his report about the Italian boardinghouse.

What can one make of this? A tentative explanation might be that he left his family and the familiar ethnic milieu in the Upper Peninsula before there was any consciousness-raising among the working-class Swede Finns. His physical separation probably led to accelerated acculturation. It is not necessary to know whether he is generalizing, romanticizing, or trivializing; the story is his interpretation of his past. It is an affirmation of his identity as a working American whose parents came from Finland and, unlike him, spoke Swedish and broken English. Despite a childhood of struggle and poverty, he has succeeded. His life story explains what he had to overcome. He measures his success in terms of his children: professionals doing very well in this adopted land of their grandparents.

Arvid Asplund's story is familiar in that it is about working-class Finnish immigrants; it is unique in that as a working man he wrote it.[4]

YVONNE HIIPAKKA LOCKWOOD
Michigan State University

NOTES

1. Anders M. Myhrman, "The Finland-Swedish Immigrants in the U. S. A.," in *Old Friends—Strong Ties,* ed. Vilho Niitemaa et al. (Turku: Institute for Migration, 1976), 181–204.

2. Tom Sandlund, "Patterns and Reasons in the Emigration of Swedish Finns," in *Finnish Diaspora* I, ed. Michael G. Karni (Toronto: Multicultural History Society of Ontario, 1981), 215–29.

3. Yvonne R. Lockwood, *The Burgenland Croats: Oral Tradition and Historical Process* (Ph.D. diss., University of Michigan, 1979). Jeff Titon, "The Life Story," *Journal of American Folklore* 93, no. 369 (1980):276–92; and Richard Dorson, who touched on this in many of his writings. See *American Folklore and the Historian* (Chicago: University of Chicago Press, 1971) and *Folklore: Selected Essays* (Bloomington, Ind.: Indiana University Press, 1972).

4. Some, of course, have written their life stories, but their numbers are few. See Reino Hannula, *Blueberry God* (San Luis Obispo, Calif.: Quality Hill Books, 1979), which is as much a Finnish-American history as his life story, and Ruth Engelmann, *Leaf House* (New York: Harper Row, 1982). Also of interest is the manual for documenting Finnish family life: Carl Ross and Velma Doby, *Handbook for Doing Finnish American Family History* (Minneapolis: Minnesota Finnish American Historical Society, 1980).

Contributors

Arvid Asplund retired in 1973, and was thus free to write the life story that appears in this volume of *Folklife Annual*. He lives in Two Rivers, Wisconsin.

Sally Banes is a critic and historian of dance and performance art. Currently a Mellon Fellow in Theatre Arts at Cornell University, she is also the performance art critic for the *Village Voice*, a senior critic for *Dance Magazine*, and the editor of *Dance Research Journal*. She is the author of *Terpsichore in Sneakers: Post-Modern Dance* (1980) and *Democracy's Body: Judson Dance Theater 1962–1964* (1983) and coauthor of *Fresh: Hip Hop Don't Stop* (1985).

Elena Bradunas was a folklife specialist in ethnic studies at the American Folklife Center from 1977 until 1985. She now lives in Hawaii.

Beverly W. Brannan is curator of documentary photography in the Prints and Photographs Division of the Library of Congress. She is coauthor of *A Kentucky Album: F. S. A. Photographers in Kentucky, 1935–1943* and served as guest curator of "Things As They Were, F.S.A. Photographers in Kentucky, 1935–1943," a photography exhibition that toured Kentucky from 1984 through 1986.

Horace P. Beck is the author of *Folklore and the Sea* (1973; 1983) and of numerous articles, both on the subject of North American Indian lore and on the sea. Dr. Beck has hunted whales in the West Indies and the Kingdom of Tonga, and collected marine lore in the Old World, North America, and in the Pacific.

Jane C. Beck is state folklorist for the Vermont Council on the Arts. She has collected life stories in the Lesser Antilles and in Vermont.

John Cohen is professor of visual arts at the State University of New York, College at Purchase. He has been visiting Qeros to record music and to make films and photographs since 1956, and his film *Qeros: The Shape of Survival* was shown on PBS's "Nova" in 1979. Mr. Cohen was a founding member of the New Lost City Ramblers, a musical group that performed traditional American music for twenty years. He has annotated ten field recordings of folk music for Folkways records, written many articles for *Sing Out* magazine, and produced eleven films about traditional music in the United States, Britain, and Peru. The events described in his article for *Folklife Annual* occurred during the filming of *Mountain Music of Peru*, which was made with the support of a Guggenheim Fellowship and with the cooperation of AeroPeru.

Carl Fleischhauer is a folklife specialist at the American Folklife Center, where he oversees the creation and use of still photographs, sound recordings, motion pictures, and video recordings.

He is coeditor (with Terry and Lyntha Scott Eiler) of *Blue Ridge Harvest: A Region's Folklife in Photographs* (1981) and editor of a laser videodisk entitled *The Ninety-Six: A Cattle Ranch in Northern Nevada* (1985).

Lauri Honko is professor of folkloristics and comparative religion at the University of Turku and, since 1972, director of the Nordic Institute of Folklore. He has been visiting professor at the University of California, at Los Angeles and at Berkeley. He is president of the Finnish Literature Society and of the Finnish Society for the Study of Comparative Religion, and the editor of *Folklore Fellows' Communications*, *Temenos*, and *Studia Fennica*. He is the author of many publications, including *Geisterglaube in Ingerland* (1962), and the editor (with V. Voigt) of *Genre, Structure, and Reproduction in Oral Literature* (1980) and *Adaptation, Change, and Decline in Oral Literature* (1981). Professor Honko's article for *Folklife Annual* is based on a paper he delivered at a symposium on the *Kalevala* sponsored by the American Folklife Center, January 24, 1985.

Edward D. (Sandy) Ives is professor of folklore, chairman of the Anthropology Department, and director of the Northeast Archives of Folklore and Oral History at the University of Maine, Orono. He is the author of a number of biographies, including *Joe Scott: The Woodsman-Songmaker* (1978).

Yvonne Hiipakka Lockwood is Michigan folklife specialist, a position supported by the National Endowment for the Arts at the Michigan State University Museum and the Cooperative Extension Service. She has lectured and written many articles on ethnic identity and foodways and is working currently on a book to be titled *The Burgenland Croats: A Model in Folk History*. Dr. Lockwood's article for *Folklife Annual* is based on a paper she delivered at a symposium on the *Kalevala* sponsored by the American Folklife Center, January 24, 1985.

Roger E. Mitchell is professor of anthropology and folklore at the University of Wisconsin-Eau Claire. He is the author of *George Knox: From Man to Legend* (1968), *I'm a Man that Works* (1978), *The Press, Rumor, and Legend Formation* (1979), and *From Fathers to Sons: A Wisconsin Family Farm* (1984).

Barry Lee Pearson is associate professor of English at the University of Maryland. He is the author of *"Sounds So Good to Me": The Bluesman's Story* (1984) and is working currently on a study of the art and lives of two Virginia bluesmen.

Jeff Todd Titon is associate professor of music and associate professor of English at Tufts University, and adjunct associate professor of music at Brown University. His publications on the subject of folklife autobiography include "The Life Story," *Journal of American Folklore* 93 (1980): 276–92; the record album *Powerhouse for God* (1982); and *Worlds of Music* (1984).

William A. Wilson is chairman of the English department and director of the Folklore Archives at Brigham Young University. He has served as editor of *Western Folklore*, director of the Folklore Program at Utah State University, president of the Folklore Society of Utah, and chairman of the Folk Arts Panel of the National Endowment for the Arts. He is on the board of directors of the Utah Arts Council and the executive board of the American Folklore Society. Professor Wilson is the author of *Folklore and*

Nationalism in Modern Finland (1976). His article for *Folklife Annual* is based on a paper he delivered at a symposium on the *Kalevala* sponsored by the American Folklife Center, January 24, 1985.

Juha Y. Pentikäinen is chairman of the Department of Comparative Religion at the University of Helsinki. He is the editor of *Folk Narrative Research* (1976) and the author of *Oral Repertoire and World View: An Anthropological Study of Marina Takalo's Life History* (1978).

Claudine Weatherford served as research associate and contributing author for the Library of Congress's Farm Security Administration—Office of War Information anniversary project. An anthropologist and a folklorist, she is currently writing a biography on genre painter Queena Stovall.

Publications of the American Folklife Center

Blue Ridge Harvest: A Region's Folklife in Photographs

By Lyntha Scott Eiler, Terry Eiler, and Carl Fleischhauer. 115 pp. (S/N 030-000-00127-3) $6. Available from the Superintendent of Documents, U.S. Government Printing Office, Washington, D.C. 20402. Check or money order payable to the Superintendent of Documents must accompany order.

A look at the landscape, communities, and religion of the men and women who live along the Blue Ridge Parkway.

Buckaroos in Paradise: Cowboy Life in Northern Nevada

By Howard W. Marshall and Richard E. Ahlborn. 120 pp. (reprint) $15.95. Available from the University of Nebraska Press, Sales Department, 901 North 17th Street, Lincoln, Nebraska 68588.

A publication to accompany the Smithsonian exhibit "Buckaroos in Paradise," including an essay on buckaroo life, a catalog of exhibit artifacts, and numerous photographs.

Children of the Heav'nly King: Religious Expression in the Central Blue Ridge

Edited and annotated by Charles K. Wolfe. Two discs and a 48-page illustrated booklet (AFC L69/70). $14. Available from the Library of Congress, Recording Laboratory, Motion Picture, Broadcasting, and Recorded Sound Division, Washington, D.C. 20540. Checks payable to the Library of Congress must accompany orders.

Cranberries

32 pp. $5. Available from the Library of Congress, American Folklife Center, Washington, D.C. 20540. Checks payable to the Library of Congress must accompany orders.

Cranberry recipes collected during the American Folklife Center's 1983 Pinelands Folklife Project in New Jersey, illustrated with full-color photographs.

Cultural Conservation: The Protection of Cultural Heritage in the United States

By Ormond Loomis. 123 pp. (S/N 030-000-00148-6) $4.50. Available from the Superintendent of Documents, U. S. Government Printing Office, Washington, D.C. 20402. Check or money order payable to the Superintendent of Documents must accompany order.

A report on the means of preserving intangible features of the nation's cultural heritage, with an appendix that traces the history of relevant legislation and a bibliography.

Ethnic Recordings in America: A Neglected Heritage

Edited by Judith McCulloh. 269 pp. (S/N 030-001-00098-2) $13. Available from the Superintendent of Documents, U. S. Government Printing Office, Washington, D. C. 20402. Check or money order payable to the Superintendent of Documents must accompany order.

A collection of essays on the history and current status of the ethnic recording industry, with numerous illustrations and an index.

The Federal Cylinder Project: A Guide to Field Cylinder Recordings in Federal Agencies

Available from the Superintendent of Documents, U.S. Government Printing Office, Washington, D.C. 20402. Check or money order payable to the Superintendent of Documents must accompany order.

VOLUME 1, INTRODUCTION AND INVENTORY, *by Erika Brady, Maria La Vigna, Dorothy Sara Lee, and Thomas Vennum, Jr. 110 pp. (S/N 030-000-00153-2) $8.50*

Introductory essay that describes the project and an indexed listing by collection of more than ten thousand field-recorded wax cylinders for which preservation tape copies exist at the Library of Congress.

VOLUME 2, NORTHEASTERN INDIAN CATALOG, *edited by Judith A. Gray;* SOUTHEASTERN INDIAN CATALOG, *edited by Dorothy Sara Lee. 432 pp. (S/N 030-000-00167-2) $14.*

Sixteen collections from northeastern Indian tribes, including the oldest collection of field recordings (the 1890 Passamaquoddy) and large collections of Chippewa, Menominee, and Winnebago music recordings made by Frances Densmore; and six collections from southeastern Indian tribes, the largest of which is the Densmore Seminole collection.

VOLUME 8, EARLY ANTHOLOGIES, *edited by Dorothy Sara Lee, with a foreword by Sue Carole De Vale. 96 pp. (S/N 030-000-154-1) $8.*

Describes Benjamin Ives Gilman's cylinder recordings from the 1893 World's Columbian Exposition and the "Demonstration Collection" edited by Erich Moritz von Hornbostel and issued by the Berlin Phonogramm Archiv shortly after World War I.

Watermelon

By Ellen Ficklen. 64 pp. $10. Available from the Library of Congress, American Folklife Center, Washington, D.C. 20540. Checks payable to the Library of Congress must accompany orders.

History, facts, and lore of the watermelon, along with numerous recipes. Illustrated in color and black and white.

The following publications are available free of charge from the Library of Congress, American Folklife Center, Washington, D.C. 20540.

American Folk Architecture: A Selected Bibliography

By Howard W. Marshall, with the assistance of Cheryl Gorn and Marsha Maguire. 79 pp.

Articles and books on theory and general topics, antecedent references from the British Isles, and resources dealing with specific regions of the country.

American Folk Music and Folklore Recordings 1983: A Selected List

An annotated list of thirty-one 1983 recordings selected because they include excellent examples of traditional folk music.

American Folklife Center

A general brochure on the center.

Archive of Folk Culture

A general brochure on the archive.

El Centro Americano de Tradición Popular

A Spanish translation of the Folklife Center's general brochure.

Folk Recordings: Selected from the Archive of Folk Culture

Brochure and order form

Folklife Center News

A quarterly newsletter reporting on the activities and programs of the center.

Folklife and Fieldwork: A Layman's Introduction to Field Techniques

By Peter Bartis. 28 pp.

An introduction to the methods and techniques of fieldwork.

An Inventory of the Bibliographies and Other Reference and Finding Aids Prepared by the Archive of Folk Culture

Information handout listing research materials at the archive.

Tradición popular e investigación de campo

A Spanish translation of *Folklife and Fieldwork.*

Traditional Crafts and Craftsmanship in America: A Selected Bibliography

By Susan Sink. 84 pp.

An indexed bibliography citing Library of Congress call numbers, produced in cooperation with the National Council for the Traditional Arts.